和果子
WAGASHI

东京艺术之旅
TOKYO ARTRIP

〔日〕美术出版社书籍编辑部　编著

崔江月　译

中信出版集团 | 北京

前言

旅行指南系列《东京艺术之旅》每册一个主题，带你从日本文化、艺术及设计的角度畅游东京。每册均有不同的艺术之旅顾问登场，本册以和果子为主题，第一章由点心研究专家福田里香带我们了解学习和果子的品类，第二章的顾问是和果子店 wagashi asobi 创始人之一的稻叶基大，《东京艺术之旅》的编辑团队在第三章中亲自为我们探店，"生活的器具 松野屋"的老板松野弘则是第四章的旅行顾问。这几位常住东京、大家一致认可的和果子忠实爱好者，给读者提供了"东京和果子赏玩之旅"的路线建议，以及不可错过的私藏店铺。

Introduction

TOKYO ARTRIP is a series of guidebooks about Tokyo. Each playful, walking spot introduced in each edition is selected from the perspective of Japanese culture, art & design. Several ARTRIP ADVISERS appear in each edition. In this wagashi – traditional Japanese confectionary, the following 4 ARTRIP ADVISERS appear in the book; Ms. Ricca Fukuda who is a Sweets Specialist (PART 1); Mr. Motohiro Inaba who is one of co-owners of "wagashi asobi" (PART 2); The editors team of the "TOKYO ARTRIP" (PART 3) and Mr. Hiroshi Matsuno who is the owner of "Tools for everyday use - MATSUNOYA" (PART 4). In this book, we take you to "playful, wagashi spots in Tokyo" recommended by these 4 wagashi lovers who live in Tokyo.

© Wagashi asobi

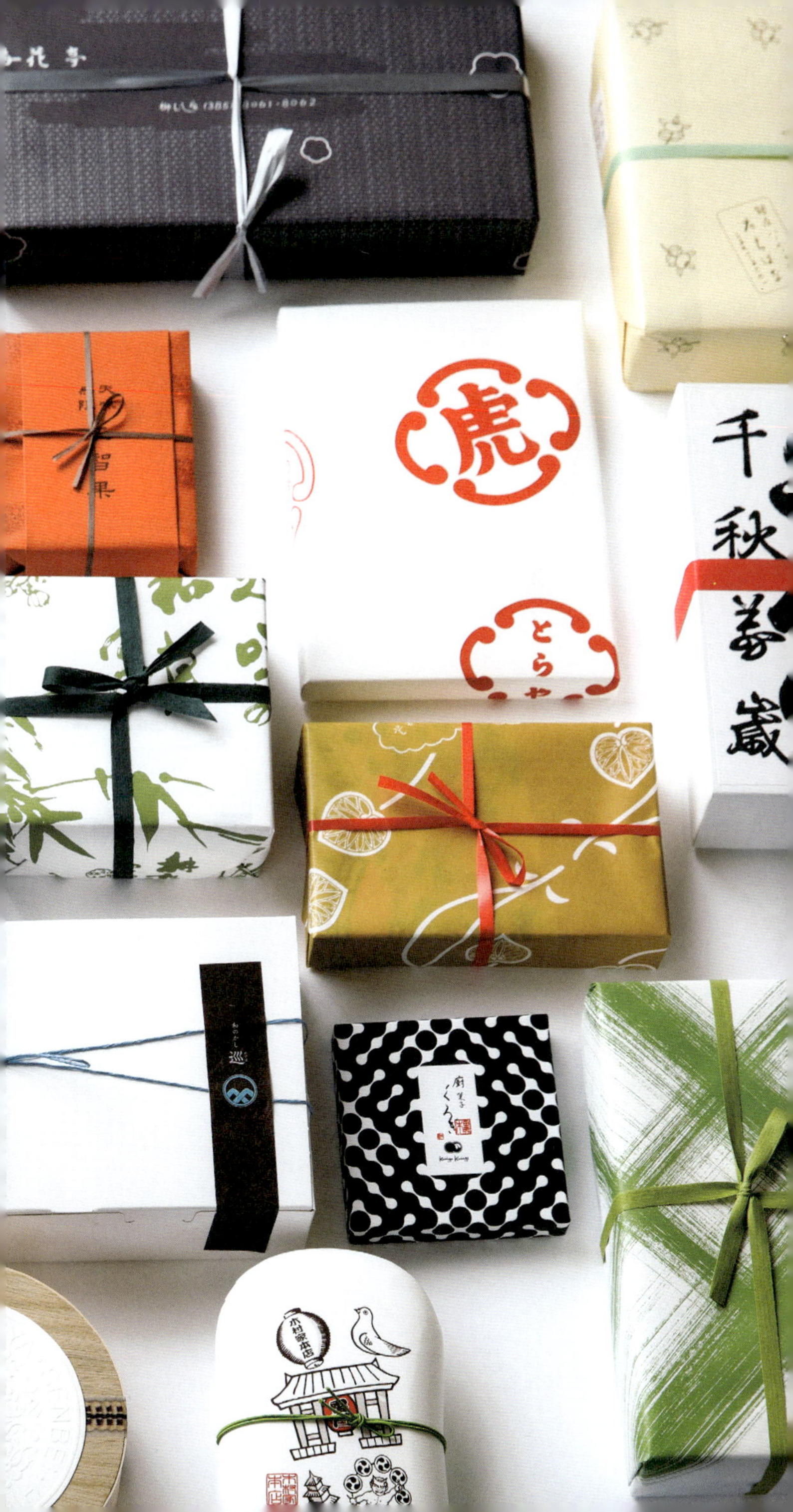
虎
とらや
千秋萬歳

目录

第一章 … 8
老店名点

1. 和果子铺笹间 … 10
2. 桃林堂青山表参道总店 … 13
3. 言问团子 … 16
4. 坂口 … 18
5. 橘 … 20
6. 长门 … 22
7. 长命寺樱饼 … 26
8. 虎屋东京中城店 … 28
   - 虎屋工坊 … 41
   - 虎屋果子屋 … 47

第二章 … 52
小小和果子铺里的招牌点心

9. 空也 … 54
10. 小笹 … 56
11. 一元屋 … 58
12. 汤岛花月 … 60
13. 银座松崎煎饼 … 62
14. wagashi asobi … 64
15. 金太郎饴糖总店 … 69

第三章 … 74
和果子的新浪潮

16. HIGASHIYA man … 76
17. 和果子 结 … 82
18. 和果子工坊 丝 … 86
19. 竹野和萩饼 … 88
20. 厨点心黑木 … 90
21. 和果子 巡 … 93
22. 白黑 … 97

- 和果子小知识 … 48
- 浅草寺百味供养会的和果子伴手礼 … 50
- 点心屋九道 … 100
- 花家 … 120
- 小百科 … 123

第四章 … 102
平民街的和果子

- 浅草寺商业街人形烧店铺 … 104
23. 木村家总店 … 107
    - 鸽子标识的木村家人形烧总店 … 108
    - 梅林堂总店 … 108
    - 三鸠堂 … 109
    - 龟屋 … 109
24. 清寿轩 … 110
25. 浪花家总店 … 112
26. 舟和雷门店 … 114
27. 梅花亭 … 116
28. 寿堂 … 118

符号说明 (时)营业时间 (电)电话 (休)休息日 (费)门票 (址)地址 (交)交通路线 (网)网址

※ 价格全部不含税。
※ 书中内容基于2017年11月信息。

CONTENTS

PART_1 — 8

HISTRIC CONFECTIONERS

1. **OKASHIDOKORO SASAMA** — 10
2. **TOURINDO AOYAMAOMOTESANDO HONTEN** — 13
3. **KOTOTOIDANGO** — 16
4. **SAKAGUCHI** — 18
5. **TACHIBANA** — 20
6. **NAGATO** — 22
7. **CHOUMEIJI SAKURAMOCHI** — 26
8. **TORAYA TOKYO MIDTOWN** — 28
   - **TORAYA KOBO** — 41
   - **TORAYA KARYO GOTENBA** — 47

PART_2 — 52

ONE OF A KIND PETIT WAGASHI

9. **KUUYA** — 54
10. **OZASA** — 56
11. **ICHIGENYA** — 58
12. **YUSHIMA KAGETSU** — 60
13. **GINZA MATSUZAKISENBEI** — 62
14. **WAGASHI ASOBI** — 64
15. **KINTAROUAMEHONTEN** — 69

PART_3 — 74

THE NEW WAVE OF WAGASHI

16. **HIGASHIYA man** — 76
17. **WAGASHI YUI** — 82
18. **WAGASHIKOBO ITO ito** — 86
19. **TAKENO TO OHAGI** — 88
20. **KURIYA KASHI KUROGI** — 90
21. **WANOKASHI MEGURI** — 93
22. **SHIROIKURO** — 97

PART_4 — 102

WAGASHI IN DOWNTOWN TOKYO

- **SENSOU-JI NAKAMISE** — 105
23. **KIMURAYAHONTEN** — 107
   - **HATONOMARUKU NO KIMURAYA NINGYOUYAKI HONPO** — 108
   - **HONKE BAIRINDOU** — 108
   - **MIHATODOU** — 109
   - **KAMEYA** — 109
24. **SEIJUKEN** — 110
25. **NANIWAYAHONTEN** — 112
26. **FUNAWA KAMINARIMON** — 114
27. **BAIKATEI** — 116
28. **KOTOBUKIDO** — 118

- **TRIVIA ON WAGASHI** — 49
- **HYAKUJYU EVENT AT SENSOU-JI** — 50
- **KASHIYA-KOKONOTSU** — 100
- **HANAYA** — 120
- **GLOSSARY** — 123

Icon Description (H) Hours of Operation (T) Telephone Number (C) Closed Days (F) Admission Fee
(Ad) Address (Ac) Access (U) URL

※All prices include sales tax.

※All information contained in this book are as of November, 2017.

第一章

老店名点

HISTORIC
CONFECTIONERS

第一章

老店的名点就像一架时空机，
带人尝遍一座城市的多重历史味道

福田里香女士在东京经常光顾的点心铺，大部分都是有着悠久历史的老店铺。"点心原本是供奉神明的供品，后来发展出平民也能享受的门前果子和茶会果子，流传到现在。长久以来保留了传统的配方制法，代代传承下来的点心铺的名点，就像是一架时空机，能够带人开启一段穿梭历史、回到过去的时空之旅，可以使我们感受到味觉以外的文化魅力。"日本全国，到处都有这样可以体会历史韵味的点心铺，当然东京有着其特有的历史味道。"即便店铺改造，或周边的风景变换，属于江户时代的和果子的味道不曾改变。如果时间合适，推荐大家体验一下在浅草寺举行的与和果子颇有渊源的百味供养会。"

Historic confectioner's traditional wagashi
are time machine
Enjoy rich history of iconic wagashi in different places

Wagashi (traditional Japanese confectionary) stores where Ricca Fukuda frequently visits in Tokyo, are often well-established stores with a rich history. "Most wagashi are originally created as offerings to Shinto Gods and Buddha, and later transformed as snacks for ordinary people, called monzengashi or sweets for tea ceremony. Those wagashi are inherited to the present day. Well-known wagashi which have kept their recipes for a long time and properly inherited till now, are like a time machine. Wagashi are fascinating to enjoy not only for their flavor but also find myself traveling back in time." She also says there are other wagashi stores all over Japan that tell their long, rich histories, and of course, in Tokyo there are wagashi stores with their unique own histories. "Although some stores have been renovated or the scenery been changed, a nostalgic retro atmosphere remains along with their wagashi. If you have time, I would like you to experience Hyakumi-kuyoue, at Sensouji."

ARTRIP ADVISER
艺术之旅顾问

福田里香
Ricca Fukuda

武藏野美术大学出身的点心研究家。除了食谱和食物评论书《漫画厨房》以外，还有多本著作。经常在 Instagram（照片墙）上分享关于和果子之类甜品的想法。

Sweets specialist who graduated from Musashino Art University. Author of recipe and food review book *Manga Kitchen* and many more. She is sharing her own concept "enjoy sweets and wagashi for breakfast" in her Instagram.

❶ 和果子铺笹间（神保町）

打开格子门，店内的气氛十分安静，外面世界的喧嚣好像一下子就消失了。店铺创建于1934年，位于神保町，当时的店内设置了茶室作为接待间，客人在品茶的同时，师傅们会在茶席上制作配食的和果子。店铺改建之后，仍然保留了这个古朴的设计，将商品陈列在昭和风情的柜台上。四位点心师傅制作的和果子，每一款都是倾心之作。创始至今始终如一的味道，吸引了大批顾客光顾。在这里，你会不由得在座席上正襟危坐，体味古老而美好的恬静之感。

(时) 9:30—18:00　(电) 03-3294-0978　(休) 星期天、节假日　(址) 千代田区神田神保町1-23　(交) 都营地铁新宿线、三田线、地铁半藏门线神保町站步行5分钟　(网) www.sasama.co.jp/

❶ OKASHIDOKORO SASAMA (JINBOUCHOU)

As you open the lattice doors, a dignified atmosphere instantly erases the outside bustle. Built in 1934, this Jinbouchou store had a *chashitsu* (a traditional tea room) acting as a reception room and has been serving beautiful wagashi perfectly matched to the tea ceremony. Even after the original building was renovated, wagashi items have been arranged the same way inside the original show case. Beautiful sets of Japanese sweets are created by four wagashi artisans with full craftsmanship. Many *chajin* (tea masters) have been constantly visiting this pristine wagashi store since it was initially established, and you will straighten your posture and experience wabisabi (a nostalgic feeling).

(H) 9:30-18:00　(T) 03-3294-0978　(C) Sundays and Holidays　(Ad) 1-23 Kanda Jinbouchou, Chiyoda-ku　(Ac) 5-min. walk from Jinbouchou Station (Toei-Shinjuku Line, Mita Line or Hanzomon Line)　(U) www.sasama.co.jp/

第一章

时令生果子

在茶会上和抹茶配食的代表性生果子。名字和造型多以季节为主题,整体感觉精美细致,赏心悦目。左上角是求肥(用糯米粉加砂糖等制成的饼皮)制作的"初秋",左下角是红豆沙内馅的练切点心"鸡冠花"(白豆沙馅加白玉粉做成外皮的和果子),右上角的"萩之户"是用白大豆和红豆制成的羊羹。右下角的"桔梗"是用大粒红小豆的带皮儿豆馅做出来的蒸制糕点。每个月会准备六款出品。(1个340日元,2个盒装810日元起)

SEASONABLE WANAMAGASHI

Traditional *namagashi* (fresh Japanese sweets) are served with matcha in the tea ceremony. Each namagashi come with a seasonal motif. The naming and appearance are simply beautiful. "Shosyu" made of *gyuhi* (sweetened soft mochi) (upper left), "Keitou" *nerikiri* (white bean based dough) with smooth textured *an* filling (lower left), "Haginoto" *yokan* (sweet red bean jelly) with white and red beans (upper right), "Kikyo" steam cake with *Dainagon red bean* (premium red bean) filling (lower right). Six different types of cakes are available each month at OKASHIDOKORO SASAMA. (¥340/pc, ¥810 & up/box of 2)

OKASHIDOKORO SASAMA

时令干果子

充分体现了日本纤巧精细之美的干果子。保质期有五天，比生果子耐放一些。州滨（将大豆烘烤以后磨成粉，混合砂糖成馅）制成的"栗子"，以洋菜粉、白砂糖、红糖为原材料制作的"桔梗"，北海道产的芸豆混合麦芽糖、白面豉酱、大米等材料制成的"芒草"。每一个都选用了最好的原材料。每月推出六款极具季节感的产品，是别的店铺找不到的纯手工出品。（100克1050日元，盒装1600日元起）

SEASONABLE OHIGASHI

Ohigashi (dry Japanese confectionary) expressing the delicate beauty of Japan. It can be stored for 5 days which is longer than namagashi. "Chestnut" made with Suhama, "Bellflower" made with kanten (agar), white sugar and black sugar. "Japanese silver grass" made with Ootebou kidney beans produced in Hokkaido, starch syrup, white bean paste and rice. All are made from the finest quality natural ingredients. Six seasonable ohigashi delicately crafted by hand are introduced every month at SASAMA.(¥1,050/100g, ¥1,600 & up/box)

第一章

❷ 桃林堂青山表参道总店（青山）

"桃林堂"总店在 1925 年于大阪创建。其特色是"风土果子"，采用不同的土地气候孕育出来各具特色的食材制作而成。店铺面向着青山大道，门面窗户都是落地玻璃，里面售卖的是具有历史内涵的独创性的和果子。品类除了基本商品之外，在不同季节还提供不同的限量商品，每一款都凝聚了匠人的心血，顾客可以从中选择。店里面还展示售卖陶艺家的作品，可以搜寻与和果子搭配的小物件。

(时)星期一 10:00—17:00 星期二至星期日 10:00—19:00　(电)03-3400-8703　(休)1 月 1 日—1 月 3 日　(址)港区北青山 3-6-12 Hulic 青山大楼 1F　(交)地铁银座线、千代田线、半藏门线表参道站步行 1 分钟　(网)www.tourindou100.jp/

❷ TOURINDO AOYAMAOMOTESANDOHONTEN (AOYAMA)

Wagashi made with natural ingredients grown from the natural essence of different lands and climates, are called "climate confectionary". This glass-walled building facing Aoyama-Dori serves the unique original wagashi with a long history. In addition to standard items, seasonal items are also available as limited editions, and you can enjoy choosing your favorites. Art work made by potters are displayed at the store and you can purchase some accessories suitable for the Japanese sweets.

(H) Tue-Sun 10:00-19:00, Mon 10:00-17:00　(T) 03-3477-8703　(C) January 1 to 3　(Ad) 1st floor Hulic Aoyama Building, 3-6-12 Kita-aoyama, Minato-ku　(Ac) 1-min. walk from Omotesando Station (Tokyo Metro Ginza Line, Chiyoda Line or Hanzomon Line)　(U) www.tourindou100.jp/

TOURINDO AOYAMAOMOTESANDOHONTEN　13

五智果

"款冬绿,莲藕白,人参红,金橘黄,无花果黑",五智果的名字来源于代表五种智慧的五智如来,选用新鲜的蔬菜和水果,保留了食材原本的风味和形状,撒上白糖晾晒而成。只采用严格挑选的日本本土食材。除了此款红盒装(无花果、洋梨、莲藕、八朔柑、款冬)以外,还有黄盒和绿盒装。(1盒951日元、礼品盒装1404日元起)

GOCHIKA

"Blue of Butterbur" "White of Lotus Root" "Red of Carrot" "Yellow of Kumquat" and "Black of Fig". Named after Gochi Nyorai (five Buddha statues representing Five Different Wisdoms of Buddha), Gochika is made with fresh vegetables and fruits coated with sugar. Each ingredient is carefully selected in Japan. In addition to the red box (figs, pears, lotus root, hassaku orange, butterbur), yellow and green boxes are available as well. (¥951/box, ¥1,404 & up/gift box)

水羊羹

NAMAMIZUYOKAN

装在千代纸盒子里面,是只有四厘米宽的方形水羊羹。水羊羹将红豆的美味最大限度地释放而出,口感十分软滑,带着淡淡的甜味。抹茶的原材料是白小豆。宇治抹茶的苦涩恰如其分地溶解其中,味道十分淡雅。这里的水羊羹是 5 月— 9 月夏季限量商品。礼品盒装很适合用来送给同事。(红小豆口味 1 个 270 日元、抹茶口味 1 个 303 日元、礼品盒 2 420 日元起)

4cm square-sized petite Mizuyokan fits in a *chiyogami* (traditional Japanese paper) patterned small box. You will enjoy a natural sweetness and the refreshing light taste of azuki beans, as they are not reheated, in order to retain the natural flavor of azuki beans. Matcha is made with white beans. A hint of bitterness of Uji matcha harmonizes perfectly with the elegant sweetness. This limited summer item is available at the store only from May to September. The gift box is a perfect present for your superiors. (¥270/red bean, ¥303/matcha, ¥2,420 & up/gift box)

TOURINDO AOYAMAOMOTESANDOHONTEN

❸ 言问团子（向岛）

"言问团子"创建于江户末期，店名取自文人在原业平所作的和歌。商标的灵感来源于和歌里的蛎鹬。从创业开始，喜欢团子和茶道的客人络绎不绝地前来，很多文化名人常常光顾，是一间有着悠久历史的老店。用签子串起来的团子的味道，并没有随时代的变迁而流失，保持了创业之初的风味。在店铺里面，可以品尝到静冈出产的山根茶和三种可爱的团子套餐。在去隅田川散步的途中买上一串边走边吃，一边欣赏自然风光，感受时光的静好，一边品味着最高级的味道，十分惬意。

(时) 9:00—18:00 (电) 03-3622-0081 (休) 星期二（月末休星期二、星期三）(址) 墨田区向岛 5-5-22 (交) 东武伊势崎线东京天空树站步行 12 分钟或都营地铁浅草线浅草站步行 15 分钟 (网) kototoidango.co.jp/

❸ KOTOTOIDANGO (MUKOUJIMA)

Established in the late Edo period, Kototoidango originates from a poem by Ariwara no Narihira, a Japanese poet. Miyako-dori ("seagull" shown on his poem) is used as trademark of the store. Many patrons and cultural figures gathered and enjoyed this iconic *dango* (a sweet Japanese dumpling made of rice flour) and tea. The dango that are not on a skewer have had the same taste since it was first established. Inside this store, you can enjoy a set menu of Yamane tea from Shizuoka Prefecture and three different adorable dumplings served on the original plate. You will enjoy the passing of time and the exquisite flavor, while walking along the Sumida River and experiencing the different scenery of each season.

(H) 9:00-18:00 (T) 03-3622-0081 (C) Tuesdays (Tue and Wed at the end of the month) (Ad) 5-5-22 Mukoujima, Sumida-ku (Ac) 12-min. walk from Tokyo Skytree Station (Tobu-Isezaki Line) /15-min. walk from Asakusa station (Toei-Asakusa Line) (U) kototoidango.co.jp/

第一章

言问团子

打开浅绿色的包装纸,三种颜色的团子整整齐齐排列其中,让人食欲大开。其中两种是将米粉搓成团,用"红豆馅"和"白芸豆馅"包成。而青黄色的团子,是用栀子将糯米团染色后,裹入青梅。食材全部选用日本本土原料。大小刚好一口,入口香软糯滑,甜度比较低。保质期只有一天,需当天享用。(1盒6个,1260日元起)

KOTOTOIDANGO

When you unwrap the bright green wrapping paper, you will be thrilled to see three different colors of dumplings neatly arranged. Red bean and white bean fillings are wrapped with shinkomochi made of rice flour. Yellowish green dumpling called Aoume (green plum) is a miso paste filling wrapped with mochi colored with gardenia pigment. All ingredients are safely produced in Japan. This bite-size dumpling has a soft and natural sweetness. Also, its smooth texture is exceptional and will satisfy customers. They are best when consumed on the same day of purchase. (¥1,260 & up/box of 6)

KOTOTOIDANGO

❹ 坂口（九段）

位于市之谷地区一口坂的尽头，靖国大道上，将江户时代的味道原原本本传承下来的煎饼专卖店。造型古朴，让人怀念的柜台上，摆放着五六十种之多的霰饼、柿饼。这里的煎饼以 100 克为单位进行售卖，计量方法保留了旧习惯。周到而细致的服务让人心情愉悦。该店创建于 1952 年。味道、品质始终如一，吸引了大批常客。还有根据不同季节制作的火柴、日历等周边赠品，收集起来也很有乐趣。

⓽ 星期一至星期五 9:30—19:00 星期六 9:30-17:30　⓮ 03-3265-8601　⓴ 星期日、节假日　ⓐ 千代田区九段北 4-1-5　㊋ JR 市之谷车站、地铁有乐町线、南北线、都营地铁新宿线市之谷车站步行 4 分钟　㊺ www.stage9.or.jp/sakaguchi/

❹ SAKAGUCHI (KUDAN)

Located on the Yasukuni Dori coming from Hitokuchizaka in Ichigaya, SAKAGUCHI is a specialty store of traditional rice crackers, having had the same taste since the Edo period. 50 to 60 kinds of *arare/kakimochi* (baked or fried glutinous rice crackers) are beautifully lined up in a wooden showcase, reminiscent of the Edo period. Items sold in units of 100 grams is an old fashioned selling by measure style. A sophisticated and meticulous manner of service makes customers feel comfortable. Established in 1952, SAKAGUCHI is popular among business customers because of its unchanged authentic flavor and quality. Customers can also enjoy the collective items such as seasonal themed matches, calendars and drawstring pouches free of charge.

(H) Sun-Fri 9:30-19:00, Sat 9:30-17:00　(T) 03-3265-8601　(C) Sundays and Holidays　(Ad) 4-1-5 Kudankita, Chiyoda-ku　(Ac) 4-min. walk from Ichigaya Station (JR Line, Yurakucho Line, Nanboku Line or Toei-Shinjyuku Line)　(U) www.stage9.or.jp/sakaguchi/

第一章

京锦

打开复古怀旧风格的铁盒,映入眼帘的是装的密密层层的海苔煎饼。这种俏皮有趣的排放方法是上一代店主设计的用来做伴手礼的专用包装。煎饼原材料是糯米加了少量酱油制成。煎饼的大小刚好一口。保质期一个月。不能一次性吃完也没关系,盒里装有小袋子,用来分赠给别人做小礼物也很适合。(一罐4320日元)

KYONISHIKI

When you open a retro chic tin, *nori senbei* (rice crackers wrapped with seaweed) tightly packed in the tin will jump out at you. This playful packaging was originally created by the previous owner as a gift box. Glutinous rice is used to make these bite sized rice crackers, with a lightly added soy flavor. Best consumed within one month of purchase. It comes with small sachets for repackaging into smaller sizes so that you can share them with someone, in case you cannot finish them by yourself. (¥4,320/tin)

SAKAGUCHI

❺ 橘（银座）

银座八丁目的小巷子里，静静地伫立着一家花林糖（油炸糖点心）专卖店"橘"。这家店自落成开业后，从未迁移。店门装饰有点像料埋店，店内布局很紧凑，没有浪费一点空间。打磨得闪闪发亮的罐装样品摆放在陈列架上，还有极具历史感的收银台静静伫立在店内。还没开门就有顾客过来排队，一位出来了，另一位再进去，保留着浓厚的传统气息。店铺没有网站，网购和邮购都行不通。除了这里哪儿都买不到，所以，还是享受一下老老实实排队等候的乐趣吧。

(时) 星期一至星期五 11:00—19:00、星期六 11:00—17:00 (电) 03-3571-5661 (休) 星期日、节假日 (址) 中央区银座 8-7-19 江安大楼 1 层 (交) JR 东海道线、山手线、横须贺线新桥站步行 5 分钟 (网) 无

❺ TACHIBANA (GINZA)

Located quietly behind a narrow alley of Ginza 8-chome, TACHIBANA is a well-established specialty store of *karinto* (deep-fried flour-based dough coated with brown sugar). When you step into the entrance, resembling a traditional Japanese restaurant, you are presented with a compact and minimal concept store and you will see beautifully polished sample tins neatly displayed on shelves and a counter table engraved with a rich history. Customers lining up before the opening hour are served one at a time. One of the Japanese modest customs remains unchanged at this store: As one customer finishes purchasing and comes out from the entrance, another one goes in. There is no store website, therefore online shopping or mail order are not available. Customers can only purchase the items in-store, but they are worth patiently waiting for.

(H) Mon-Fri & day before Holidays 11:00-19:00; Sat 11:00-17:00 (T) 03-3571-5661 (C) Sundays and Holidays (Ad) Eyasu Building 1st Floor, 8-7-19 Ginza, Chuo-ku (Ac) 5-min. walk from Shinbashi Station (JR Tokaido Line, Yamanote Line or Yokosuka Line) (U) N/A

第一章

花林糖

灰绿色罐子上面的图案是飞舞着的橘子花，里面装了两种花林糖——胖乎乎的"小胖"和细条的"小枝"。涂了好几层糖浆的花林糖，看上去如同打磨过的宝石一样，光泽诱人。两种花林糖各有各的味道和口感，对比起来也很有乐趣。包装纸和纸袋都统一采用橘子花图案。作为用来表达诚心的伴手礼很受欢迎。（长方形罐装1号1512日元起）

KARINTO

Inside a grayish green colored tin with flower patterns of Tachibana, there are two kinds of karinto: a thick round shaped "Koro" and a thin twig-like "Saeda". Delicately coated with layers of glazed sugar, the beautifully shined surface resembles a polished jewel. It is fun to compare the two different flavors and textures of Koro and Saeda. The wrapping paper and paper bags are also printed with the same flower motif of Tachibana. Packaged with those original paper bags, they make an excellent gift with which you can convey your true heart. (¥1,512 and up/square tin No.1)

TACHIBANA 21

❻ 长门（日本桥）

日本桥地区在江户时代作为东京的商业、文化中心而繁荣起来，长门坐落在日本桥的一角。其历史可以追溯到日本战国时代，曾经作为德川七代将军吉宗御用的和果子店备受信赖，至今约有三百年的历史。店铺入口旁的橱窗上有1941年的和果子店铺人气排名表，该店傲然居于横纲（用日本相扑运动员的级别代表排名的高低，横纲是最高级别）。因经历了多次灾难，店铺里面的旧物件已被烧毁，但秘传的味道却由历代匠人传承了下来。现在的店面是1989年重建的，里面古朴的木制柜台仿佛在无声地述说着历史的厚重沧桑。

(时)10:00—18:00 (电)03-3271-8662 (休)星期日、节假日 (址)中央区日本桥3-1-3 (交)JR东京站八重洲北口步行2分钟或地铁银座线、东西线、都营地铁浅草线日本桥站步行1分钟 (网)nagato.ne.jp/

❻ NAGATO (NIHONBASHI)

Nihonbashi once flourished as a commercial and cultural hub of Tokyo during the Edo period. Located in one part of Nihonbashi, NAGATO was established during the Sengoku Period (Warring States Period). As a purveyor to Yoshimune Tokugawa, the seventh general of the feudal government, it became a favorite wagashi store with over 300 years of history. You can see the ranking list in 1941 attached to the show window beside the entrance. It is dignified as a grand champion. Although the previous store's details were burned out due to repeated disasters, the secret recipe has been inherited by the artisans. While the store was rebuilt in 1989, the old wooden showcase remains at a store that tells its rich history.

(H)10:00-18:00 (T)03-3271-8662 (C)Sundays and Holidays (Ad)3-1-3 Nihonbashi, Chuo-ku (Ac)2-min. walk from JR Tokyo Station Yaesu Exit /1-min. walk from Nihonbashi Station (Tokyo Metro Ginza Line, Tozai Line or Toei-Asakusa Line) (U)nagato.ne.jp/

第一章

深山风卷什锦

形状如同小小的花瓣,一口大小的烤制点心,把百宝盒装得满满当当的。"风卷"在和果子中是指"像被风吹过一般,许多种和果子混合在一起",也就是我们常说的"什锦"的意思。深山风卷什锦里有甜煎饼之类的烤制点心,形状颜色都十分漂亮,很有品位。豆子和芝麻的点缀使其口味丰富多样,让人不知不觉就送到了嘴边。这款极具高级感的罐装什锦和果子,保质期有一个月。(罐装 2 700 日元起)

MIYAMAFUKIYOSE

A treasure box full of petal-like, bite-sized baked confectionary. Fukiyose literally means blown up by wind and gathered, and generally is an assorted petite higashi. However, only baked confectionary like sweet flavored rice crackers are sold as fukiyose at this store. Their shape and color are chic and elegant. Ingredients such as beans and sesame seeds are incorporated well into the dough and provide a variety of rich flavors. You won't be able to stop eating them. Items kept in this gorgeous designed tin will last for one month. (¥2,700 & up/with tin)

NAGATO

半生果子

半生果子造型取材于各式各样的风物，颜色繁复，绚丽多彩。黄豆粉做的"毛豆"，琼脂做的"小鲇鱼"、"夏日花火"，柚子馅做的"柚子新绿"等，有模具做出来的也有手工制作的，式样繁多，变化多端。这种点心口感柔和，一般会根据季节的不同变换品类。保质期一周。这款点心采用贴了千代纸的特质木盒包装，当作礼物送人非常受欢迎。（盒装2000日元、千代纸盒装特小号3000日元起）

HANNAMAGASHI

Hannamagashi (semi-fresh Japanese confectionary) has different shapes and colored features; "Edamame" made with *Kinako* (roasted soybean flour), "Ayu" and "Senkohanabi" made with agar jelly, and "Yuzu no aoba" made with Yuzu bean paste. These are made through special molds or are handmade, and customers can enjoy many variations of them. These gentle melt-in-your-mouth items are changed every season. Best consumed within one week of purchase. A signature wooden box decorated with *chiyogami* is also a popular item as a present. (¥2,000/with box, ¥3,000 & up/Chiyogami special box(small))

葵最中

以德川家家徽冬葵的叶子为外形设计灵感。包装纸和盒子，还有点心薄酥饼皮的双面，都印了冬葵叶的图案。薄酥饼皮加了黑芝麻烤制，里面包裹着小仓红豆馅，一口下去，高级的口感让人心满意足。店铺的地下层和二楼的工厂里面有和果子的手工制作专区，每天都可以在这里买到新鲜的产品。在悠长的历史中传承下来的味道，如今依然充满生机。（1盒6个，1380日元起）

AOIMONAKA

Leaf of Aoi (hollyhock) is a crest of the Tokugawa family. As proof that the store was allowed to use this crest, two leaves of hollyhock are printed on wafers of *monaka* (a wafer cake filled with bean paste). Monaka wafers are made with a mixture of pastry flour and black sesame seeds. *Ogura an* (smooth an) is sandwiched between the two thin crisp wafers. You can enjoy a sophisticated flavor. They are handmade at their kitchens so that customers will enjoy freshly made monaka every day. Authentic flavors inherited from the past remain unchanged at this store today. (¥1,380 & up/box of 6)

❼ 长命寺樱饼（向岛）

隅田川附近正宗的"樱饼"发祥店。1717 年，创始人将河边堤坝上的樱花叶子盐渍后在其中放入了香甜的糯米，开始在长命寺的门前售卖。这里的樱饼传承至今已有三百年历史，选材严格，不使用任何添加物。店内设有堂食专区，可以品尝刚出炉的新鲜樱饼。樱花季节可以外带。这里的樱饼是历史与大自然的馈赠物，樱饼一直深受日本民众的喜爱，很多美食家特意来到这里，一饱口福。

(时) 8:30—18:00　(电) 03-3622-3266　(休) 星期一　(址) 墨田区向岛 5-1-14　(交) 都营地铁浅草线、地铁半藏门线、京成押上线、京成成田快线、东武伊势崎线押上站步行 15 分钟　(网) www.sakura-mochi.com/

❼ CHOUMEIJI SAKURAMOCHI (MUKOUJIMA)

Located by the Sumida River, this specialty store has an ancient and honorable origin of "Sakuramochi". In 1717, the founder initially made the rice cakes wrapped with a salt-preserved cherry leaf and began to sell them in front of the gate of CHOUMEIJI temple. This sakuramochi has a rich history of over 300 years, is made with carefully selected ingredients, and does not contain any additives. You can enjoy the refreshing flavor of freshly made sakuramochi at an eat-in section within the store. Takeaway items are only available during the cherry blossom season. Many gastronomes have been constantly visiting this iconic store. This one-of-a-kind sweet has been popular among many people for a long time as a gift of history.

(H) 9:30-18:00　(T) 03-3622-3266　(C) Mondays　(Ad) 5-1-14 Mukoujima, Sumida-ku　(Ac) 15-min. walk from Oshiage Station (Tokyo Metro Toei-Asakusa Line, Hanzomon Line, Keisei-Oshiage Line, Keisei Narita Skyaccess / Tobu-Isezaki Skytree Line)　(U) www.sakura-mochi.com/

长命寺 樱饼

把三片樱花叶一片一片揭开，樱饼优美的模样就显现出来了。伊豆的松崎町生产的盐渍樱花叶，可以防止樱饼干燥，并且可以保存樱饼内馅的甜美幽香之气。建议将樱花叶剥下后再享用。因每日制作的数量有限，想买来做伴手礼的话就要提前预约了。（1个200日元、6个盒装1350日元起、10个篮装2500日元起）

CHOUMEIJI SAKURAMOCHI

As you peel three cherry leaves one by one, a delicate rice cake with a thin mochi pops out. Locally grown cherry leaves in Matsuzaki-cho of Izu are salt-preserved for 6 months and are used to wrap mochi, in order to prevent them from becoming dry while also providing the light aroma and flavor of a cherry leaf itself. Its recommended to peel the leaves carefully. Limited quantities are made per day therefore advance orders are advisable if you wish to take some home. (¥200/pc, ¥1,350 & up/box of 6, ¥2,500 & up/ basket of 10)

❽ 虎屋东京中城店（六本木）

虎屋创建于室町时代的后期，原本是在京都，1869 年日本迁都东京的时候一起随迁了过来，作为和果子界的"泰斗"广受关注。2007 年开业的东京中城店，为大众展现了这间百年老店的另一面。店铺门口的门帘彰显着虎屋品牌的标识，里面是简单的商品陈列，店铺设计以白色为基调，十分具有现代风格。里面还设有专门介绍日本传统文化的展示厅。随着时代的发展，向新的时代发起挑战，虎屋将继续书写它的历史。

⊛11:00—21:00　⊛03-5413-3541　⊛元旦　⊛港区赤坂 9-7-4 D-B117 东京中城店 Galleria B1　⊛地铁日比谷线、都营地铁大江户线六本木站直达或地铁千代田线乃木坂站步行 3 分钟或地铁南北线六本木 1 丁目站步行 10 分钟　⊛www.toraya-group.co.jp

❽ TORAYA TOKYO MIDTOWN (ROPPONGI)

Originally established in Kyoto during the late Muromachi period, TORAYA moved to Tokyo in 1869 at the same time as the relocation of the capital to Tokyo. Since then, as an authority on wagashi, TORAYA continues to attract many customers. The Tokyo Midtown store was opened in 2007 and introduced a new form of Japanese culture fused with modern times. There is a dignified *noren* (a shop curtain hanging at the entrance), a simple display of a large range of items, and a white-themed modern interior. It also comprises a gallery that introduces Japanese culture. New approaches reflected by modern life have become a part of their rich history now.

(H)11:00-21:00　(T)03-5413-3541　(C)January 1　(Ad)D-B117, B1 Floor Tokyo Midtown Galleria, 9-7-4 Akasaka, Minato-ku　(Ac)Direct access from Roppongi Station (Tokyo Metro Hibiya Line, Toei-Ooedo Line) / 3-min. walk from Nogizaka Station (Chiyoda Line), 10-min. walk from Roppongi 1-chome Station (Nanboku Line)　(U)www.toraya-group.co.jp/

第一章

虎屋馒头

随着冬季的到来，虎屋馒头作为时令商品出现在店里。虎屋馒头历史悠久，据说虎屋馒头的制法是在公元1241年由从中国回来的圣一国师流传下来的。这款独具匠心、一代一代传承下来的点心，外皮原材料使用糯米和酒曲，经过长时间发酵，风味醇厚，带有独特的酒香。馒头没有使用任何添加剂，每日制作的数量也有限。回家后重新蒸一下再慢慢享用，柔滑上乘的风味在舌尖扩散。（每个400日元、礼品盒装6个2549日元）

TORAYA-MANJU

As winter arrives, a seasonal item *Toraya Manju* is lined up at Toraya. The recipe was brought to Japan by a Buddhist monk named Shoichi Kokushi upon his return from China in 1241. This *manju* (steamed bun with an filling) has been passed on from generation to generation over the decades. Glutinous rice and malted rice are used to make the dough and let it sit for a few days so that it creates a rich flavor and a unique aroma from malted-rice. No additives are used. Limited quantities are made per day. The best way to enjoy this smooth and sophisticated flavor is to steam it again. (¥400/pc, ¥2,549/box of 6)

TORAYA TOKYO MIDTOWN

羊羹

日本传统的和果子之一——羊羹。右边是正统的"夜梅",切口上的红小豆颗粒就像那暗夜里绽开的梅花,口感充实。在江户时代就留有制作羊羹的记录。左边是寓意了四季更迭风景的时令羊羹"千岁菊"。象征着长寿不老的菊花,代表秋天的色彩。中等大小让顾客可以同时享用多种味道。(夜梅1条1512日元,千岁菊1条1944日元)

YOKAN

Yokan is one of the most traditional Japanese sweets. The standard yokan "Yoru no Ume"(right). When sliced, the azuki beans evoke the glimmer of white plum blossoms in the dark night and it has a thick spongy texture. Yokan was first recognized in the Edo period according to Toraya's archival documents. The seasonal yokan "Chitosegiku"(left). The color of the chrysanthemum is used as a symbol of eternal youth and longevity together with the autumn-themed colors. Both are medium sized so that customers can enjoy their favorite size or thickness. (¥1,512 each/Yoru no Ume, ¥1,944 each/Chitosegiku)

和三盆糖制五色丝

WASANBONTOU GOSHIKIITO

"五色丝"始于1992年,其命名来自五色丝线的传说。古时候,传说女子想要学好纺织可以在七夕这一天将五色丝线装饰在小竹子上,就可以实现愿望。这款点心将五色丝线所蕴含的美好愿望与在平安时代象征贵妇阶层的装饰物"编结"造型相结合。上图从上到下分别是"薄荷""生姜""梅子肉""柚子""肉桂"。五色丝精美而纤巧,各不相同的形、色、香、味,不随波逐流,不受时代影响,是和果子中的名品。(1盒1728日元)

In 1992 , *goshikiito* was created to pray for weaving and sewing skills by hanging five different colored threads on the tip of bamboo sticks on *Tanabata* (a star festival held on July 7th) and people believed those threads made their wishes come true. It is named after those threads in five colors. During the Heian period, the "knot" skill was recognized as a status of cultured ladies; therefore the "knot" was designed as the motif. From the top, "Hakka", "Ginger", "Plum", "Yuzu", and "Nikkei". These beautiful and delicate shapes, colors, aromas and flavors have remained unchanged through the years and continue to satisfy many customers. (¥1,728/box)

TORAYA TOKYO MIDTOWN

虎屋的时令生果子图鉴
SEASONABLE NAMAGASHI

以四季更迭的风物为主题，
震撼五感的饮食艺术

生果子色泽漂亮，造型精美，魅力非凡。江户时代（1603—1867），随着茶道文化的推广，生果子以京都为中心发展起来，为贵族所推崇。因为使用了昂贵的白砂糖，在当时被称为"上果子"，是难以入手的高级品。四季迥异的造型灵感来自日本丰富多样的自然风土。果子外形主题有植物、动物、自然、风景等等，全都是古时候就深受日本人喜爱的、常常出现在歌谣和绘画里面的内容。既有具体形象的造型，也有看不出什么头绪的抽象造型。点心名字一般来自《古今和歌集》《源氏物语》等古典文学。即便是抽象意蕴主题的生果子，只要听到点心名，就能联想到制作者想要表达的意境。让我们一起来品味一下"饮食的艺术"吧。

Seasonal motifs featuring different seasonal images
Food art satisfies your five senses

Namagashi attracts many people with its wide range of beautiful colors and designs. During the Edo period (early 1700s to late 1900s), the roots of namagashi were developed in Kyoto along with the Japanese culture of tea ceremony. Since white sugar, an expensive ingredient at that time was used to make namagashi, it was a luxury item called "high grade confectionary." These seasonal designs are inspired by a well-endowed climate and the natural environment of Japan. The motif is an expression of plants, animals, nature or landscapes, or an inspiration of poems and pictures which many people are familiar with. These motifs differ from abstract to specific design. *Kamei* (a name given to each wagashi) is influenced by classical Japanese literatures such as "A Collection of Ancient and Modern Japanese Poetry" and "The Tale of Genji", and the Japanese antique art. When you see an abstract designed namagashi and find out the kamei, you will feel the spirit of the artisan. Let us introduce some "food art" in the next section.

第一章

※ 照片上的点心，一部分现已不售卖。
※ Some of the items in this picture are not available.

TORAYA TOKYO MIDTOWN

霜红梅

寒意残存的早春时节，在寒风料峭中早早绽开的梅花上，落下了霜露。红色的求肥（制作和果子的一种材料）包裹着麦糖馅，形状饱满的红梅花瓣上面，撒着雪白的糯米粉，营造落霜的感觉。

SHIMOKOBAI

Around early spring with a lingering cold, SHIMOKOBAI expresses a plum blossom blooming among the frosty cold scenery. This round shaped plum blossom is made with white bean paste wrapped with a rosy-pink colored gyuhi, and coated with *shinbikiko* (lightly roasted, finely ground rice flour), which resembles frost.

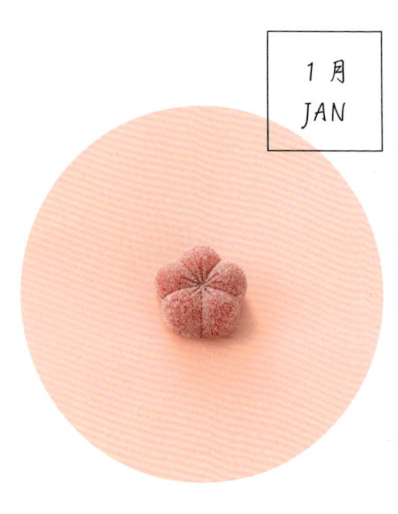

1月
JAN

2月
FEB

莺饼

象征着春意盎然的点心。求肥包裹着豆沙内馅，两端收起来，上面撒上绿色的豆粉。求肥和莺哥绿的豆粉将简单抽象化的黄莺姿态和羽毛颜色勾画在人们眼前。

UGUISUMOCHI

UGUISUMOCHI is made with *gozen an* (high quality smooth red bean paste), wrapped with gyuhi. It is pinched at both ends of a mochi shell and then coated with a greenish colored kinako. The symbolic color of *uguisu* (Japanese bush warbler) and its wings are expressed with the ingredient itself, such as gyuhi and kinako.

※ 生果子的外观颜色每年会不同。
※ The color of namagashi may vary from year to year.

第一章

手折樱

3月 MAR

蕴含了日本人对樱花的喜爱之情。"樱花盛开的美丽姿态如同在讴歌春天一样,这样的美景我不忍自己一个人欣赏,用手折了下来想带回去给妻子和孩子们一同欣赏。"这款点心做工纤巧精细,色彩十分漂亮。

TAORIZAKURA

TAORIZAKURA embodies Japanese people's deep love for sakura (cherry blossoms). The message: "The beauty of cherry blossoms blooming which celebrate the arrival of spring is not something to keep to myself. I would like to pick a small branch and take it home to share the beauty with others" is beautifully interpreted in this item. This delicate design and color is very beautiful.

4月 APR

八重霞

八重霞在日语中表示层层的春日彩霞。使用湿米粉做成,分别染成绿、红、黄三种颜色压制而成。这个创意让人想起春天里开放在彩霞之下的野花。是一款表达了亲近自然的心情、造型高雅而优美的作品。

YAEGASUMI

YAEGASUMI means the layered spring mist rising in the air. YAEGASUMI is made with *shippun* (a strained and steamed mixture of rice flour and bean paste), and three layers are dyed with green, red and yellow. Its design creates an impression of how the spring wildflowers are shrouded in the mist. This is an elegant wagashi that conveys a respect for the beauty of nature.

TORAYA TOKYO MIDTOWN

菖蒲馒头

将碾碎的山药捏成团，搓成椭圆形后蒸制而成。上面烙有菖蒲花的印花，再用笔一片一片细心描绘出往上伸展的叶子。

AYAMEMAN

Manju called Jouyo manju is made with grated tsukuneimo (a kind of yam) formed in an oval shape and then steamed. A brand of iris flower (ayame) is burnt in this manju, and the leaves are carefully drawn one by one using a paintbrush.

5月
MAY

6月
JUN

初萤

葛粉制的饼皮内包着生地（竹芋粉），像水边飞来飞去的萤火虫一样从半透明的饼皮中透出淡淡的光芒。人们把夏天第一次出现的萤火虫叫作"初萤"，这款点心的名字就来自于此。是一款富有诗意，体现了夏日之景的作品。

HATSUBOTARU

Yellow bean paste wrapped with arrowroot jelly expresses a firefly flying by the waterside and glowing in the faint light. It was named after "Hatsubotaru", fireflies that appeared for the first time in the summer. This item makes you picture a poetic sentiment of the summer.

第一章

7月
JUL

新叶浮影

金鱼,在俳句等日本古典文学里面是用来指代夏天的季节语。这款点心刻画了漂浮在水面上的绿叶影子,以及金鱼若隐若现畅游其中的样子,甚至还透着阵阵清凉的气息。色泽漂亮,晶莹剔透,带着冰凉感,在夏日非常受欢迎。

WAKABAKAGE

Goldfish is a season word reflecting the summer used in haiku etc. WAKABAKAGE is made with kanten and expresses a goldfish swimming in and out of the shadow of fresh green leaves floating on the surface. It has been a popular item with beautiful colors and refreshing coolness.

8月
AUG

观世水

室町幕府的第三代将军足利义满赠送给能乐的观世大夫(观世流派掌门人)的宅子里有一口叫作观世井的水井。这款点心正是将井里的旋涡的形状具象化后呈现出的作品。

KANZESUI

There was a water well called Kanze-i at the house which Yoshimitsu Ashikaga, Muromachi shogunate's third shogun, provided to Noh actor Dayuu Kanze (head master of Kanze family school of Noh). The shape of KANZESUI is based on the design of a whirlpool built up in the well.

TORAYA TOKYO MIDTOWN

9月
SEP

栗鹿之子

让人想象到硕果累累的秋天的"栗鹿之子"。以鹿背上的白色斑纹（鹿的斑点）为形象构思，将蜜渍的金灿灿的栗子装饰在内馅上。栗子需要一片一片小心翼翼地手工贴上去，是非常花心思的作品。

KURIKANOKO

An imagined fruitful autumn, KURIKANOKO is inspired by white patches of a deer's back, and made with circular shaped bean paste, and decorated with shiny chestnuts preserved in honey. Carefully arranged by hand, each chestnut around the bean paste is a beautiful work of craftsmanship.

10月
OCT

山路之锦

一款以红叶为原型制作的色彩绚丽的点心。因为红叶鲜明的色彩以及华丽的纹路模样就像是织出来的提花织锦。点心名的寓意就来源于此。里面是加了肉桂的豆沙馅，味道独特。

YAMAJI NO NISHIKI

Gorgeous colors are the expression of leaves turned red and yellow and overlapped with each other. Its vividness is often compared to a brilliant pattern of a woven figured textile. YAMAJI NO NISHIKI is named after this pattern and is made with gozen *an* mixed with nikkei.

虎屋东京中城店

第一章

11 月
NOV

初霜

初霜至，秋渐深。用虎屋自家生产的米糕捏成山茶树叶一样的形状，上面撒上糯米粉，营造出一种仿佛一口气就可以被吹走的初霜残叶的风情。

HATSUSHIMO

When the first frost appears, the autumn season advances. A camellia-shaped thick leaf is made with *uiro* (steamed rice cake) and sprinkled with shinbikiko. HATSUSHIMO, which literally means a first frost, creates a quaint atmosphere as if it will disappear if you blow at it.

12 月
DEC

深山之雪

深山寂处雪皑皑。白色的部分代表雪，黑色的部分代表土地和森林。原料是山芋和甘栗。这款点心的配色给人深山寂寞之感，是一款带有沉静感而寓意颇深的和果子。

MIYAMA NO YUKI

A scene of a deep mountain covered with snow early in the winter. This item is made with *kinton* (pureed bean). Minced white kinton resembles snow and minced black kinton resembles a mountain surface and forests. Its deep color expresses the quiet solitude of Miyama mountain and gives you a calm and nostalgic feeling.

TORAYA TOKYO MIDTOWN

虎屋工坊

一日旅行
去探访神圣的虎屋工坊

Day trip from Tokyo
A must-visit Toraya Kobo

第一章

虎屋工坊

富士山脚下御殿场市,是虎屋工坊的所在之地。创始人希望还原最初的和果子铺,让和果子与地域风土相融合,2007年静悄悄地在御殿场开了这家工坊。工坊占地面积广阔,约18 500平方米,四周围绕着自然景色。在日式庭院里散步之后,可以到工坊内部观看师傅在厨房认真制作点心的模样,再饱尝一顿新鲜出炉的美味和果子,满口留香。虎屋工坊可以满足你一次奢侈的味蕾体验,在微风吹拂的庭院内,品尝只有此处才有的、只能"一期一会"的美味和果子。

(时) 10:00—18:00(4月至9月),10:00—17:00(10月至次年3月) (电) 0550-81-2233 (休) 星期二、年末年初 (址) 静冈县御殿场市东山1022-1 (交) JR御殿场站乘坐的士15分钟车程或自驾,从东名高速路御殿场IC第二出口出去后行驶7分钟 (网) www.toraya-kobo.jp

TORAYA KOBO

Located near the foot of Mt. Fuji, Gotemba is closely connected with TORAYA KOBO. With a concept of going back to the origin as a wagashi store, it quietly opened in 2007. These 5,600-square meter spacious premises are surrounded by the different natural scenery of each season. After enjoying a stroll in the garden, you can watch the artisans making wagashi at the workshop, and then savor freshly made sweets. "TORAYA KOBO" will fulfill such a supreme moment. Customers can enjoy the breeze blowing through the premises and relish unique wagashi available only here at TORAYA KOBO.

(H) 10:00-18:00 (April to September) 10:00-17:00 (October to March) (T) 0550-81-2233 (C) Tuesdays & the year-end and New Year holidays (Ad) 1022-1 Higashiyama, Gotemba, Shizuoka Prefecture (Ac) 15-min. by taxi from Gotemba station (JR Gotemba Line) /7-min. drive from Exit No.2 Tomei Kosoku Gotemba IC (U) www.toraya-kobo.jp/e

TORAYA KOBO

①来到入口，映入眼帘的是昭和二年（1927年）建成的原酒井家别墅的楼门。小路也保留了当时的原样，周边环绕着郁郁葱葱的竹林。

②对着花园的露天座位。坐在这里，可以一边观赏开阔的自然美景，一边品尝美味的和果子，让香甜的味道在味蕾扩散。在这个和自然融为一体的空间，可以完全放松身心，十分惬意。轻松的自助服务模式也很贴心。

③木质装修的售卖专区。柜台上摆满刚出炉的和果子，十分赏心悦目。一边挑选要在这里吃的或者打包带回家的点心，一边和店员闲聊，让人倍感温馨。

④本地农场直供的煎茶。用心冲泡，茶香浓郁醇厚，和这里制作的点心十分相配。

① A temple gate with a straw-thatched roof welcomes you at the entrance. These premises are the former Sakai family's villa built in 1927. The bamboo grove and narrow path leading to the entrance have been unchanged from the past and blend in well with the gate. ② The premium terrace seats facing the garden. While enjoying a panoramic view of natural scenery, you can savor the delicious wagashi. This open-plan tea room is well harmonized with nature and creates a relaxed atmosphere. The self-service style is also pleasant. ③ The wooden interior of the purchase area gives a cozy warmth like woods. Freshly made wagashi in the adjacent kitchen are beautifully arranged at the counter table. While customers choose their wagashi to eat-in or takeaway, they can enjoy conversation with the friendly staff. ④ This studio's original sencha is made with ingredients produced by local firms. The fragrance and rich flavor of carefully brewed sencha match perfectly with the freshly made wagashi.

第一章

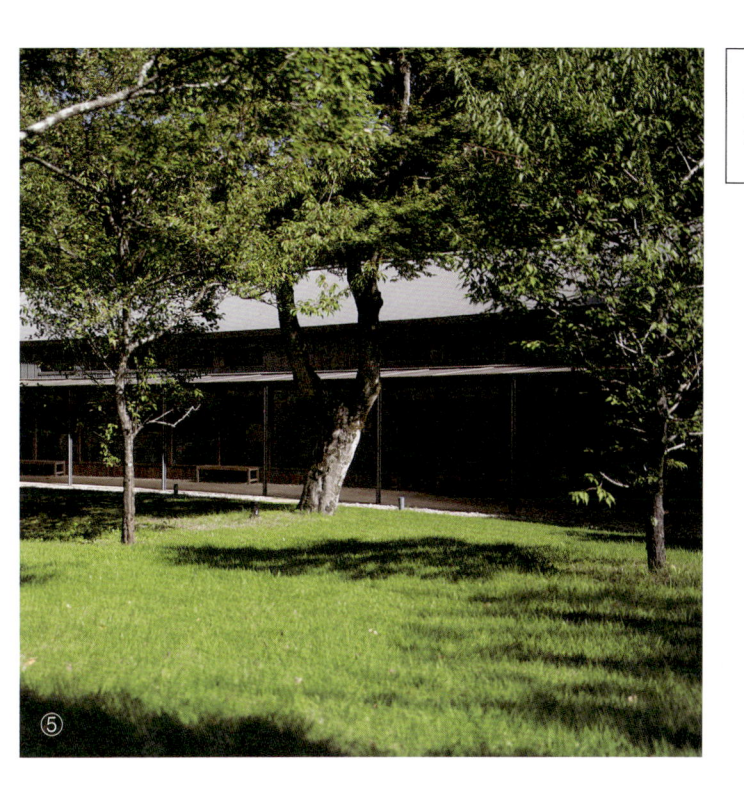

⑤建筑家内藤广设计的内庭建筑。广阔庭院内坐落着虎屋工坊,建筑的外观线条平缓而流畅。在梅花盛开的季节,清新的空气中夹杂了丝丝梅香,让人非常舒适。寒冬时节,还可以在温暖的茶室里品茶赏雪。

⑤ Designed by the architect Hiroshi Naito, the studio features a soft and smooth curve as if it wraps the spacious garden. Like in the plum blossom season, this semi-outdoor-style studio is the perfect space for customers to feel the refreshing breeze from the garden. Even in the cold of winter, the fireplace placed inside makes it cozy.

TORAYA KOBO　　　　　　　　　　**43**

①透过玻璃隔板，可以观看厨房里面制作点心的过程。里面是凝心聚力、专心制作点心的师傅们。和果子原材料以当地出产的让人放心的新鲜原料为主，也使用一些时令食材。

① Through the glass window at this kobo, customers can watch the artisans making wagashi at the workshop. They use seasonal fresh ingredients locally produced and put their hearts and souls into creating wagashi.

②全神贯注制作大福的师傅们。为了凸显糯米原本的风味，饼皮没有加糖，一边称分量，一边捻平放入馅料，再一个一个娴熟轻巧地包起来。

③用道明寺米粉和三盆糖做成的栗子糯米团。季节限定和果子使用具有季节特色的时令材料做成，根据不同的季节变换品目。

④刚做好的大福，一个接一个地被摆放在木盒子里。一眼看过去好像只是随意摆放，却又整整齐齐。不得不向用经验积累出来的匠人致敬。

⑤在180度的铜板上烤制出来的饼皮，为了加强蛋黄的风味，底料采用当地出产的"樱花鸡蛋"，一个一个烤制得蓬松饱满。师傅们连续不停的熟练技法让人忍不住屏息凝神。

② The artisans dedicated to creating *daifuku* (small round mochi with bean paste filling). In order to retain the natural flavor of Japanese glutinous rice, the mochi shell is made without sugar. They measure the mochi dough, flatten it into a thin layer and wrap it around a rolled bean paste ball one by one with brisk efficiency.

③ The process of making chestnut mochi using Doumyouji flour and *wasanbon sugar* (a fine-grained, high-quality Japanese sugar). Time-limited items made with seasonal fresh ingredients will change every season. ④ Freshly made daifuku are arranged in the wooden box. They seem to be put in carelessly, but are actually neatly arranged inside the box. The high aesthetic sense of experienced artisan is truly admirable. ⑤ Pancakes of *dorayaki* (sweet pancakes filled with an in between), baked on a 180-degree hot copper plate. Flavorful local "Sakura egg" is used to make the dough, in order to maximize the flavor of egg yolk. Pancakes are baked one by one until they become fluffy. Their skillful work with a deft motion is breathtaking.

TORAYA KOBO

新鲜出炉的铜锣烧和大福,搭配温热的煎茶一起食用,是人间极致的美味。因为工坊里面还提供简餐,有些客人把这里当成可以放松的家一样,从日出待到日落。这恰恰证明了虎屋带来的无处不在的休闲舒适感。(煎茶铜锣烧套餐、煎茶大福套餐 584 日元)

Freshly baked dorayaki and daifuku together with warm sencha are absolute heaven. There are also snack menus, so some customers stay and relax at the studio from morning till evening as if it's their second house. This is proof that customers feel their hospitality while the spirit of Toraya reaches every corner. (Sencha/Dorayaki set, Sencha/Daifuku set /¥584 each)

虎屋工坊

虎屋果子屋
TORAYA KARYO GOTEMBA

既然来到了御殿场，那就顺便到另一家"虎屋果子屋"看看。这座位于御殿场的虎屋主要工厂，于 1978 年建造完成。两年后虎屋御殿场店开业，1988 年开始售卖季节限定的羊羹"四季富士"。阳光透过落地窗洒落进来，一边眺望气魄宏伟的富士山，一边在这里品尝虎屋的绝品和果子，也可以买好打包回家。

(时) 10:00—19:00（卖场）11:00—18:30（果子屋）(电) 0550-83-6990 (休) 不固定 (址) 静冈县御殿场市新桥 728-1 (交) JR 御殿场站箱根乙女出口步行 9 分钟或自驾，从东名高速公路御殿场 IC 第 1 出口出来后行驶 3 分钟 (网) www.toraya-group.co.jp/toraya/shops/detail

In 1978 the main factory was completed in Gotemba. It opened two years later, and Toyara's season-limited "Four seasons of Mt. Fuji" has been sold since then. After looking at the majestic Mt. Fuji, enjoy their signature yokan and feel sunlight pouring softly through the glass window at the store. It is also available for takeaway as a souvenir.

(H) 10:00-19:00 (Store), 11:00-18:30 (Karyo) (T) 0550-83-6990 (C) Occasional (Ad) 728-1 Shinbashi, Gotemba, Shizuoka (Ac) 9-min. walk from Gotemba Station Hakone Otome Exit (JR Gotemba Line) / 3-min. drive from Tomei Kosoku Gotemba IC Exit No 1 (U) www.toraya-group.co.jp/toraya/shops/detail

刻画了富士山不同季节景色的羊羹："四季富士"。上图是"秋"，用暗红色和黑色的炼羊羹来表现夕阳时分漫天红霞的背景下，富士山悠然耸立的景色。（附带抹茶套餐 1404 日元）

"Four seasons of Mt. Fuji" describes the beautiful appearance of Mt. Fuji changing every season. "Mt. Fuji in Autumn" expresses the sunset in the background of dignified Mt. Fuji. It is made with dark red and black-colored neriyokan. (¥1,404/with matcha)

第一章

TORAYA KARYO GOTENBA

和果子小知识

历史

现在,一般认为以鲜果等树木的果实和水果为原材料,用大米和小米、稗子等谷物加工而成的糕点和团子,是和果子的原型。受到日本飞鸟至平安时代的遣唐使们从中国带回来的"唐点心"、镰仓至室町时代禅僧们创作的点心、战国和江户时代初期从葡萄牙传来的"南蛮点心"这三类点心的影响,从江户时代起日本人开始研发并制作具有日本特色的和果子。

节日活动

和果子,与自古传下来的时令传统节日有着很深的关系。不同的节日需要有不同的和果子搭配,正月的"花瓣饼",3月女儿节的"菱饼",3月和9月祭祀先人的"萩饼",5月儿童节的"柏饼"和"粽子",6月夏日驱邪的"水无月"等等。还有意喻消灾祈福的叫作"嘉祥"的节日(6月16日),在当天有品尝华丽精美的和果子以消灾的习俗。

种类

和果子的种类,根据含水量可以分成三大类。水分比较多存放时间短的"生果子",羊羹、烤果子和最中等可以存放一周时间的"半生果子",还有干果子,水分含量比较少,经过干燥处理的砂糖点心就是这一类。

材料

以自古就生长在日本的植物原材料为主。用来做馅料的红小豆、芸豆等豆类,道明寺米粉、米粉、白玉粉(糯米粉)、寒梅粉、新粉(用粳米制作)等米粉,还有葛粉、蕨粉等等。柿子、柚子、梅子等水果类和栗子、罂粟籽、芝麻等原料也会出现。

TRIVIA ON WAGASHI

第一章

HISTORY

Wagashi originate from nuts and fruits called mizugashi. In the past, processed grain such as rice, millet, Japanese millet were used to make rice cakes and dumplings, and later they transformed to wagashi. "Chinese sweets" were brought to Japan from China by Kentoushi in the Asuka/Heian period, "Dim sum" was brought by Zen monks in the Kamakura/Muromachi period and "European sweets" were brought from Portugal in the Sengoku/Edo period. Influenced by these three kinds of sweets, during the Edo period, original wagashi were created along with the unique colors, shapes and names.

EVENT

Wagashi are strongly associated with seasonal events succeeded from ancient times. Largely known wagashi are "Hanabira Mochi" for New Year, "Hishi Mochi" for the Doll Festival in March, "Ohagi" for the equinoctial week in March and September, "Kashiwa Mochi" and "Chimaki" for the Children's Day in May, "Minazuki" for Nagoshi-no-Harae in June and others. Associated with the event called Kajo, there is a custom of eating the gorgeous wagashi on the Wagashi Day (June 16) to pray for expelling evil spirits and inviting good luck.

TYPES

Mainly wagashi are categorized into three groups in terms of the water content. "Namagashi" contains a large amount of water and has a short shelf life. "Hannamagashi" such as yokan, baked items and monaka last about 1 week. Another, the dried sugar confectionary is categorized into "higashi" which contains less water than the other two types.

INGREDIENTS

Since ancient times, the ingredients grown in the Japanese climate are mainly used to make wagashi. "Beans" are used for bean paste such as red beans. "Rice" such as Doumyoji flour, rice flour, glutinous rice flour, Kanbai flour and shinko, also, arrowroot flour and bracken flour. "Fruits" such as persimmon, citron, plum and "seeds" such as chestnuts, poppy seeds and sesame seeds are also used as ingredients.

浅草寺百味供养会的和果子伴手礼
HYAKUJYU EVENT AT SENSOU-JI

位于浅草的浅草寺，平日里会用小豆汤和干果子供奉观音。百味供养会，是每年 6 月 18 日举行的带有特别祈福意义的法会仪式。这个仪式，主要是将仿制的百种山珍海味的供品点心装在竹笼子里供奉给观音。因为供品装在竹笼子里，又叫作"笼供品"。参加祈祷礼的人，可以享用供奉后撤下来的笼供品。

At Sensoji Temple in Asakusa, *oshiruko* (sweet red bean soup) and higashi are regularly offered to the statue of the Goddess of Kannon. Every year, the ritual called Hyakumi-kuyoue is held on June 18, where people express their gratitude to the goddess. At this event, some of the "Hyakumi" that substitutes for 100 kinds of wagashi of the sea and the land, are put in bamboo baskets. These bamboo baskets are used as offerings at the Buddhist memorial service. Based on the fact that the offerings are packed into the bamboo basket, it is also called "basket offerings". Worshipers can bring home these gorgeous baskets full of wagashi if they book in advance.

用竹子编制的精巧竹笼，解开绑在上面的装饰物，编到一半的竹笼就可以打开了。里面装了煎饼、盐斧（粉糕）、饴糖等干果子。让我们怀着感恩之心，来品尝这些供品。

Higeko is a basket beautifully braided with bamboo. While you remove the decorations on the top, the middle parts are not braided so the top will smoothly open. Inside Higeko, there are different kinds of higashi, such as rice crackers, *rakugan* (a type of Japanese dried candy) and candies. You can savor the same higashi that was offered to the Goddess of Kannon with a sense of the sacred.

第

第二章

小小和果子铺里的招牌点心

ONE OF A KIND
PETIT WAGASHI

精益求精长久经营下来的店铺里的招牌商品，让人心情愉悦

wagashi asobi 是一家制作、售卖和果子的店铺（本书第64页有介绍）。创始人稻叶基大先生在开店之初，他心中就有着理想店铺的样子。"要有一道招牌商品，坚守这一样就能一直做下去，像街边的小小的和果子铺就很好。"比如，只做最中，或者只做羊羹、煎饼，不勉强扩张店面，提供一款雅致的、用心的能够成为店铺门面的商品，成为被当地人长久喜爱的存在是他的理想。"和果子作为一种想要送给别人，或者自己享用的东西，也是一种与人沟通的工具，所以能否得到人们的喜爱是我们自己制作点心、出售点心的标准。"

第二章

Store's specialty wagashi made with passion can bring us happiness

The wagashi artisan, Motohiro Inaba, had a solid image that he aimed for when he opened his business, "wagashi asobi" (p.64): "A small, neighborhood wagashi shop focusing on one particular specialty." Apparently, his ideal shop would be one that has long been loved by the locals, offering one specialized confectionery such as monaka, yokan or senbei, carefully, modestly and painlessly made. "Wagashi is a gift to be given or received. It is a kind of communication tool, so whether it makes people happy or not is how I determine which wagashi to make and buy."

ARTRIP ADVISER
艺术之旅顾问

稻叶基大
Motohiro Inaba

和前同事浅野理生一起，2011年在大田区开了这家"Wagashi asobi"。稻叶负责"香草落雁"（一种印糕），浅野负责"干果羊羹"。在世界各地开展日式点心推广活动。

Motohiro and his former co-worker back when their apprenticeship, Rio Asano, opened "wagashi asobi" together in Ota-ku in 2011. Motohiro makes "Herb Rakugan," and Rio makes "Dried Fruits Yokan." They participate in worldwide wagashi events.

53

❾ 空也（银座）

"空也最中"作为东京代表性和果子，空也店外从早上起一直排长队，非常火爆。手工制作一天能够完成的数量大概有 8000 个。即便提前电话预约购买也很难买到，需要提前几日预约。为了保持品质，店主一直坚持着当天制作的东西只在当天售卖的方针。该店一百三十年前在上野开业，1949 年转移到银座。这家位于并木大道一角的店铺，门口上方挂着显眼的门帘，在诉说着它的历史。夏季（6月—9月）和冬季（10月—次年5月）店铺会为顾客分别提供蓝色和豆沙色的包装纸，也很贴心。

(时)星期一至星期五 10:00—17:00，星期六 10:00—16:00　(电)03-3571-3304　(休)星期日、节假日　(址)中央区银座 6-7-19　(交)地铁银座线、丸之内线、日比谷线银座站步行 5 分钟，JR 有乐町站、新桥站步行 10 分钟　(网)无

❾ KUUYA (GINZA)

Early in the morning, people line up for the most reputable wagashi in Tokyo, KUUYA MONAKA. As they are handmade, about 8,000 pieces are made each day. Although they usually sell out by advance phone orders, they must all be sold on the same day to assure their quality. It is the policy passed on through generations. About 130 years ago, the original shop had opened in Ueno, and they moved to the current location on Ginza's Namiki street in 1949. The noren proudly hung on its front door shows its history. The wrapping paper is blue in summer (Jun. through Sep.) and orange in winter (Oct. through May), a form of courtesy that pleases customers.

(H) Mon-Fri 10:00-17:00, Sat 10:00-16:00　(T) 03-3571-3340　(C) Sundays and Holidays　(Ad) 6-7-19 Ginza, Chuo-ku　(Ac) 5-min. walk from Ginza Station (Tokyo Metro Ginza Line, Marunouchi Line, Hibiya Line) / 10-min. walk from Yurakucho Station or Shinbashi Station (JR Line)　(U) N/A

空也最中

KUUYA MONAKA

这款最中的名字"空也"起源于空也念佛的传说,空也两个字印在葫芦形状的饼皮上。外形小巧精致,馅料由自家手工制作,采用北海道出产的低农药红豆和白粗糖制作而成,与酥脆的饼皮十分相配。老少咸宜,是别处绝无仅有的高级品。常温避免干燥,可以保存一周。早上9点开始接受电话预约。(10个自用盒装1030日元起,礼品盒装1130日元起)

KUUYA was named after *Kuuya Nenbutsu*, a prayer to Amida Buddha recited while dancing. Its logo is on the gourd-shaped monaka. People of all ages like this small yet delightful combination of crispy toasted wafers filled with a handmade an made with reduced agrochemical red beans from Hokkaido. No other places sell their monaka. Keep it at room temperature, avoid dryness, and consume within a week. They accept phone orders from 9 am. (¥1,030 & up / regular box of 10pcs, ¥1,130 & up/gift box)

KUUYA

⑩ 小笹（吉祥寺）

这里售卖一天只能制作 150 条的珍品羊羹。为了买到这个羊羹，40 年以来客人们从早上 5 点开始在店前排起来的长队，已经成了吉祥寺的一道风景。只有约 3 平方米大小的店铺，时至今日仍坚守着上一代店主创造的"小笹的味道"。据店主说，当年不断地尝试，一直得不到上一代店主的认可。直到某天制作出来的羊羹，终于被点头说"可以了"。这样极致的如艺术品一般的羊羹，需要排长队购买也是物有所值。让人想要传承下去的独一无二的味道，就是在这样有匠人精神的店铺诞生。

(时) 10:00—19:30 (电) 0422-22-7230 (休) 星期二 (址) 武藏野市吉祥寺本町 1-1-8 (交) JR 京王井之头线吉祥寺站步行 2 分钟 (网) www.ozasa.co.jp/

⑩ OZASA (KICHIJOUJI)

Only 150 of OZASA's famous yokan are made per day. Early birds start gathering for the rare yokan in front of the 3.3m² store as early as 5 o'clock in the morning, and this has been going on for the past 40 years. Such a sight is not unusual but rather a part of daily life in Kichijouji. It proves that the very special "OZASA's taste," perfected by the predecessor, has been kept strictly the same as the original. There was innumerable trial and error before the predecessor finally nodded "yes." At that moment, the red beans shined in purple and whispered to him, recalls the owner. It is worth waiting in line for the precious, masterpiece, yokan. OZASA is where to find the one-of-a-kind confection that should be carried on to the next generation.

(H) 10:00–19:30 (T) 0422-22-7230 (C) Tuesdays (Ad) 1-1-8 Honchou Kichijouji, Musashino-shi (Ac) 2-min. walk from Kichijouji Station (JR Keio Inokashira Line) (U) www.ozasa.co.jp/

炼羊羹

外形小巧精致，色泽诱人的极品羊羹。细腻光滑的口感，让人回味无穷的甜香，一瞬间就俘获了味蕾。因为一直坚守传统的制作方法，使用低效的小锅、昂贵的木炭熬制馅料，生产量一直无法提升。要保证严格挑选的材料能够稳定供应也是一道难题。早上 8 点 15 分，一人仅能购买 3 条的预约券就售完了。(1 份 760 日元)

HONNERIYOKAN

It is a refined, small yokan with a beautifully glossy color, and definitely the best yokan of all. The smooth texture accompanied with deep sweetness is so irresistible. To maintain their tradition, an inefficiently small pot is heated with costly charcoals to cook beans. Therefore, they cannot increase the productivity. Also, it is not easy to acquire a stable supply of carefully selected ingredients. One reservation ticket lets a customer purchase up to 3 yokan. All tickets are gone by 8:15. (¥760/pc).

OZASA

⓫ 一元屋（曲町）

店内的柜台上，只摆放着父子两人合力做出来的金锷饼和最中两种和果子。1955年创业之初，店主一心想要制作品质上乘的和果子，经过无数次的研发与尝试后，创作出了一元屋特别的金锷饼。金锷饼是由发祥于京都的银锷饼演变而来的。原本是圆形的锅缘形状，传到江户后，变成四角形，格调高端起来，因而被称为金锷饼。一元屋的金锷饼，形状、大小，还有包装，都保留了创业之初的模样。繁复而独特的制作方法，传递着手工制作的温暖。附近的常客和商务顾客也比较多，想买的话需要提前预约。

㈲星期一至星期五 8:30—18:00，星期六 8:30—15:00 ㈲03-3261-9127 ㈹星期日、节假日 ㈲千代田区曲町 1-6-6 ㈹地铁半藏门线半藏门站出站直达 ㊆无

⓫ ICHIGENYA（KOUJIMACHI）

In ICHIGENYA's display cabinet, you will find only *kintsuba* (square red bean cake) and monaka, which were perfected by the owner and his father. Since its opening in 1955, they have dedicated themselves to these two specialties to ensure serving top quality wagashi, and that is how this "Kintsuba" was born. "Gintsuba", a silver (gin) cross-guard (tsuba) shaped wagashi from Kyoto, was introduced to Edo city (former name of Tokyo during 1603 to 1868). Later, it became square and was named as "Kintsuba (golden cross-guard)" to refer to its elegance. Their kintsuba is the same shape and size as the original, and they are even delicately individually wrapped just like the way it was back then. ICHIGENYA's unique recipe requires patience and has no short-cut. That's the secret of heartful satisfaction that we feel from their handmade treats. Pre-order is recommended before they are sold out because they have many regulars from the neighborhood and surrounding businesses.

(H) Mon-Fri 8:30-18:00 Sat 8:30-15:00 (T) 03-3261-9127 (C) Sundays and Holidays (Ad) 1-6-6 Koujimachi, Chiyoda-ku (Ac) Less than 1 min. walk from Hanzomon Station (Tokyo Metro Hanzomon Line) (U) N/A

第二章

特制金锷饼

饼子外披着一层薄薄的小麦面浆，方形，只有五厘米宽。将红菜豆和冰糖熬煮后，使用琼脂将馅料凝固，再沾上一层小麦粉，在铜板上煎制。要把六面都煎得均匀很考验技巧。沙沙的口感中带着淡淡咸味的颗粒馅料，口味上乘。保质期三天。还有真空包装可以作为礼品送人，保质期六天。（1 个 151 日元，6 个盒装 906 日元起）

TOKUSEI-KINTSUBA

A lightly battered, 5x5cm size block. High-quality Dainagon red bean and rock sugar are slow-cooked together and stiffened with agar. After being dusted with flour, the cubed *an* mixture is fried on the copper plate till crispy. Only experienced professionals can fry all six surfaces evenly. Enjoy the delicate taste of lightly salted *tsubu-an* (chunky *an*) jelly enhanced by a crispy bite. Kintsuba lasts for 3 days, and the vacuum-packed ones are good for 6 days if you buy them for a gift. (¥151/pc, ¥906 & up/ Box of 6)

ICHIGENYA

⓬ 汤岛花月（汤岛）

店铺的原身，是 1947 年由上上代的老板娘经营的一间小小的粗点心店。店铺结构保留了从前的样子，只在充满着人情味的汤岛开了这一家。这是一家专注花林糖七十年的专卖店。花林糖在江户时代作为平民点心广受欢迎。这家的花林糖形状朴素，滋味让人上瘾，传承现到现在始终坚守着原本的味道。点心的包装也是它的魅力之一。红色的圆柱形的罐子，不仅能够保持风味，因其形态可爱，也有很多顾客买来作为伴手礼送人。

㈠ 星期一至星期五 9:30—20:00，星期六、星期日和节假日 10:00—17:00 ㈢ 03-3831-9762 ㈣ 不固定 ㈡ 文京区汤岛 3-39-6 ㈤ JR 御徒町站步行 5 分钟或地铁银座线上野广小路站步行 3 分钟或千代田线汤岛站步行 3 分钟 ㈥ www.karindou-kagetsu.com/

⓬ YUSHIMA KAGETSU (YUSHIMA)

In 1947, YUSHIMA KAGETSU was originally started as a small candy shop by a woman who was the owner three generations ago. The shop still keeps the same structure as before in the warmhearted downtown, Yushima, and is the sole store. "Karinto" has been their specialty for 70 years. As an inexpensive snack, karinto was widely popular to common people in the Edo period. Simply formed, but addictively tasty, karinto hasn't changed till this day. The cute red round canister not only keeps karinto fresh but also is another reason why many customers buy it as a gift for special occasions.

(H) Mon-Fri 9:30-20:00 Weekends & Holidays 10:00-17:00 (T) 03-3831-9762 (C) Occasional (Ad) 3-39-6 Yushima, Bunkyou-ku (Ac) 5-min. walk from Okachimachi Station (JR Line) /3-min. walk from Ueno-Hirokouji Station (Tokyo Metro Ginza Line) /3-min. walk from Yushima Station (Tokyo Metro Chiyoda Line) (U) www.karintou-kagetsu.com/

第二章

花林糖

琥铂色的光泽十分诱人，外壳好像吹制玻璃一般光泽透亮。底料在不同油温的三只锅里炸了三次，连里面的芯都变得脆脆的，上面浇上使用独特方法熬制的糖浆。轻柔的甜味和浓郁口感共存，这样自古流传下来的美味，令人意犹未尽。（小圆罐装1998日元）

KARINTOU

Beautifully glossy, golden brown, firm and crunchy like a glass sculpture. In their special recipe, karinto dough is deep fried three times in three different pots; each of them is set at a different temperature. Fried crunchy to the center, the karinto will be coated with slow-cooked white sugar candy. A perfect combination of mild sweetness and full body flavor, which has never changed since the original, makes you come back for more. (¥1,998/ small round canister)

YUSHIMAKAGETSU

⑬ 银座松崎煎饼（银座）

1804 年，在江户文化盛行的时代，最早的"松崎煎饼"在名为三河屋的店铺诞生了。后来，店铺从鱼篮坂转移到现在总店所在的银座，店名也进行了更改。店铺在经历了关东大地震、战争后被烧毁，而最重要的制作煎饼的模具，据说被第五代家主埋在地里奇迹般保存了下来。这家店铺的招牌和果子，是叫作"三味胴"的"瓦形脆煎饼"。地下一楼是瓦形脆煎饼的专卖楼层，里面播放着细心制作煎饼过程的录像。在这家重新装修过的店铺里，慢慢地品尝自己喜欢的味道，再好不过了。

⓽11:00—20:00 ⓔ03-6264-6703 ⓗ无 ⓐ中央区银座 5-6-9 银座 F·S 大楼 1 楼 ⓙ地铁银座线、丸之内线、日比谷线银座站步行 2 分钟或 JR 有乐町站、新桥站步行 8 分钟 ⓦmatsuzaki-senbei.com/

⑬ GINZA MATSUZAKISENBEI (GINZA)

In 1804, during the time in which flamboyant Edo culture had been flourishing, the original MATSUZAKI SENBEI was established as Mikawaya (a traditional Japanese liquor store) at Gyoranzaka. Later, they moved to Ginza where their main location currently is, but the store had been destroyed multiple times by the earthquakes and the war. The fifth generation shop owner hid the most important iron senbei mold under the ground. Their first and main product was *Kawara Senbei* (roof tile shaped cookie), called "Shamido." The specialty shop of kawara senbei is on the first basement level, where customers can watch a video showing how carefully they are made. Find the one for you from various selections filling the awe-inspiring freshly remodeled store.

(H) 11:00-20:00 (T) 03-6264-6703 (C) None (except the end of year and new year) (Ad)1st Floor of Ginza F.S building, 5-6-9 Ginza, Chuo-ku (Ac)2-min. walk from Ginza Station (Tokyo Metro Ginza Line, Marunouchi Line, Hibiya Line) / 8-min. walk from Yurakuchou Station, Shinbashi Station (JR Line) (U) matsuzaki-senbei.com/

第二章

江户瓦日历

因为形似三味线的琴身,所以被命名为"三味胴",是一款甜味的瓦形煎饼。煎饼用小麦粉加入鸡蛋和砂糖烤制出来后,师傅们会在每一片上绘制江户的风情画。图画一般是四季变换的花鸟风月,纤细的美丽姿态完全就像是艺术品,让人想要慢慢欣赏后再品尝味道。(8 片盒装 1080 日元起)

EDOGAWARA KOYOMI

This sweet kawara senbei looks like the body ("dou" in Japanese) of a *shamisen*, a traditional Japanese musical instrument, which is why it was named "Shamido." It is made with flour, eggs, and sugar. Each piece has seasonal scenery of Edo city painted on by the hands of the artisans. The beautiful delicate painting is like a work of art. Take a moment to appreciate the artwork before eating. (¥1,080 & up/Box of 8)

GINZA MATSUZAKISENBEI

⑭ wagashi asobi（长原）

四位和果子师傅联手开创的店铺兼工作室"wagashi asobi"。进入店内，新鲜的香草味迎面而来。店铺以打造东京地区的传奇和果子铺为目标，同时接受国内外著名品牌委托，倾注全力制作具有收藏价值的和果子和特别订购品，如今活动的范围逐步扩大。售卖的和果子品种以羊羹和落雁为主，其宗旨是每一颗和果子都要投入情感。正是在这样的宗旨下，他们将传统和果子用全新的食材进行了演绎。简单的包装也闪耀着店铺个性。

(时)10:00—17:00 (电)03-3748-3539 (休)不固定 (址)大田区上池台1-31-1-101 (交)东急池上线长原站步行1分钟 (网)wagashi-asobi.com/

⑭ WAGASHI ASOBI (NAGAHARA)

"Wagashi asobi" is a quartet of wagashi artisans and also the name of their shop/atelier, where the fresh scent of herbs enthusiastically welcomes customers. While their passion is to be a small local wagashi shop, their business has been successfully collaborated with internationally famous brands, for which they have made specially designed novelties. Their focus is only on yokan and rakugan. Under their motto, to "put thought into each moment and each piece," they give a concrete shape to the possibility of creative wagashi using innovative ingredients. The simple package also reflects their brilliant unique character.

(H) 10:00-17:00 (T) 03-3748-3539 (C) Occasional (Ad) 1-31-1-101 Kamiikedai, Ota-ku (Ac) 1-min. walk from Nagahara Station (Tokyu Ikegami Line) (U) http://wagashi-asobi.com/

第二章

干果羊羹

当时接到外部委托要求制作可以和面包搭配的羊羹时,为了能够和面包完美搭配食用,师傅们对选材认真斟酌,制作出干果羊羹。里面加了很多干无花果和果仁,口感很独特。香滑的红豆馅100%选用北海道出产的红小豆制作,用甘蔗制成的红糖来调和甜味。羊羹既有水果的酸味,适中的甜味中,还隐隐带着一丝朗姆酒的香味,堪称绝品。(1条2160日元)

DRIED FRUITS YOKAN

For a request of a wagashi that goes well with bread, they have tested and carefully selected ingredients. This yokan has a generous amount of dried figs and nuts, so its cut surface looks quite distinctive. The smooth textured *an* is made with Hokkaido red beans and sweetened with brown sugar from sugar cane. A tartness from fruits and a mellow sweetness from *an* are assembled with a hint of rum, presenting this astonishing treat. (¥2,160/bar)

WAGASHI ASOBI

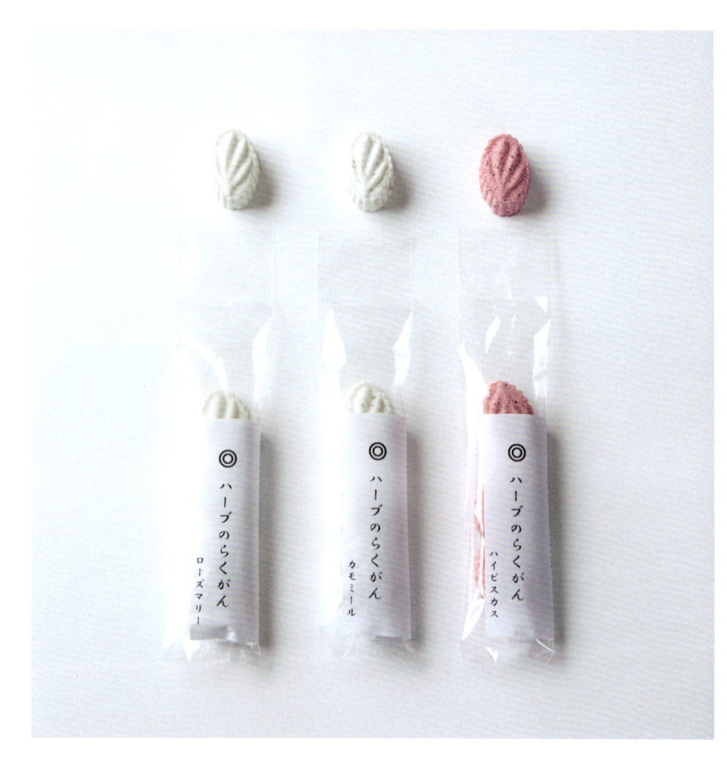

落雁

树叶形状的落雁，散发出香草的芳香。三种香草分别是和红茶很搭的迷迭香、加了粉红花瓣颜色鲜艳的木槿、柔和自然的洋甘菊。店铺出品的点心没有使用任何的添加剂和调味料，将众人熟识的西洋食材的风味巧妙地融合进日本传统点心之中。入口柔和，阵阵的自然气息让人忍不住一颗接一颗地品尝。（每款4粒装360日元）

HERB RAKUGAN

This leaf shape rakugan has a fragrant scent of Western herbs: Rosemary goes well with tea, hibiscus flower petals are used for a bright pink color, and chamomile gives a scent of gentle nature. No additives or artificial fragrances are used. They make the best use of common Western herbs to create this unique wagashi. It melts instantly in your mouth. Feel and taste the wonderful nature, one piece at a time. (¥360/assorted pack of 4pc)

wagashi asobi 的个性化定制落雁
wagashi asobi CUSTOMIZED RAKUGAN

第二章

历史悠久的最高级的钢笔品牌——万宝龙公司定制的两种落雁的木制模具。这款落雁以十厘米大小的钢笔尖端和品牌商标为设计灵感，在 2016 年圣诞节前的宣传活动中，和装在罐子里作为赠品的羊羹一起出售。

These are two wooden rakugan molds made to order for Montblanc, the historic brand of luxury fountain pens. One is a design featuring a pen nib (approx. 10cm), and the other is the brand's logo. Montblanc gave away rakugan made with these custom-made molds for their pre-Christmas promotion in 2016. They were boxed in a tin-can together with their yokan.

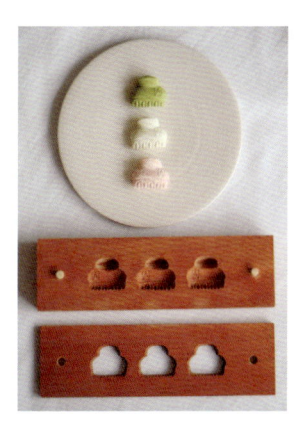

以发饰奢侈品牌——Alexandre de Paris 旗下的 VENDOME 发夹为造型的落雁和木制模具。有抹茶、迷迭香、草莓三种口味。这是 2017 年青山店开业时作为纪念礼物为品牌定制的。

Alexandre de Paris is a famous brand of luxury hair accessories. These rakugan were designed in the motif of the Vendome clip, one of their most popular products. In the picture, there are green tea, rosemary, and strawberry flavored rakugan, and the wooden mold. They were provided as gifts to celebrate their new Aoyama store opening in 2017.

WAGASHI ASOBI

金太郎饴糖总店

金太郎饴糖是怎么制作出来的?
工坊探访

How is KINTAROU-AME made?
Let's visit the factory

第二章

❶❺ 金太郎饴糖总店（三之轮）

从露天摆摊的卖糖商起家，明治时代后半期，第二代店主设计创作了东京名产"金太郎饴糖"。传说中的金太郎是个力大无穷的小孩。这款糖包含了希望孩子健康成长的愿望，商家始终坚守着自古传下来的制作方法，如今也坚持手工制作。工坊里大部分都是原创产品和定制产品，长久以来坚持使用秘传配方制作糖果。让我们一起来探访一下位于店铺二楼的工坊吧。

时 9:00—17:30　电 03-3872-7706　休 星期六（不固定）、星期日、节假日　址 台东区根岸 5-16-12
交 地铁日比谷线三之轮站步行 1 分钟　网 www.kintarou.co.jp/

❶❺ KINTAROUAMEHONTEN (MINOWA)

Their very first shop started as a candy food cart. About 100 years ago, the second-generation owner created "KINTAROU-AME," and it is now known as one of Tokyo's specialties. Kintarou, a boy representing a strong child, is the motif of this candy. Even today, they are made by hand with the traditional method, wishing that children grow up strong. They carry various originally designed candies and also accept custom orders as well. For many years at the same location, they have inherited the secret method of making these candies. Let's check out what is happening in their factory located on the second floor.

H 9:00-17:30　T 03-3872-7706　C Saturdays (occasionally), Sundays and Holidays　Ad 5-16-12 Negishi, Taito-ku　Ac 1-min. walk from Minowa Station (Tokyo Metro Hibiya Line)　U www.kintarou.co.jp/

KINTAROUAMEHONTEN

金太郎饴糖总店

第二章

工坊里面的制作工序十分紧凑,没有任何多余的工序。经验丰富的师傅们动作利落,不停地来回翻转着糖果。这个看起来巨大的糖块,是金太郎饴糖的原形。为了不让糖冷却凝固,所有的作业都要快速进行。

Tools are neatly arranged according to the manufacturing process. Experienced artisans are working very efficiently in the factory. The huge block of candy shown in this picture is the original form of the KINTAROU-AME. All procedures must be done quickly before the candy cools down and hardens.

KINTAROUAMEHONTEN

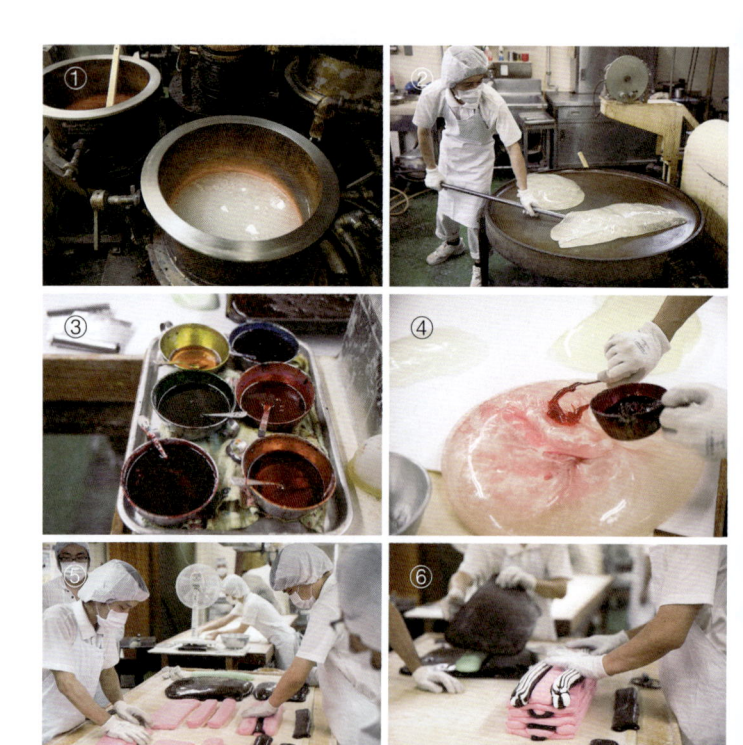

①首先要制作糖浆。在大口的铜锅里,搅拌麦芽糖和白砂糖,熬煮30分钟。

②将高温的糖浆从锅里取出来,转移到冷却板上面。将冷却到60度左右的糖坯,放到机器中冲入空气,直到颜色发白。

③染色染料有八种基础颜色。这些染料混合起来可以调出各种各样的颜色。糖果图案上浓淡层叠的颜色、细节部位的色彩都是用这些染料混合后上色而成的。

④白色的饴糖被分成不同的部分,分别上不同的颜色。粉红色是金太郎饴糖的表面颜色。为了使其上色均匀需要快速搅拌。

⑤成形之前,根据所需分量将上了颜色的坯料分切成不同大小。坯料降温冷却后会凝固,为了使不同部位保持一样的温度,需要师傅快速操作。

⑥从下往上,把不同颜色的糖坯依照需要制作的糖果的样子堆叠起来。极有经验的师傅们,能够一边翻转重重的糖块一边使其成形。

① First, in a large copper pot, starch syrup and granulated sugar are mixed and cooked for about 30 minutes. ② The hot liquidized sugar is removed from the pot and put onto a plate to cool down. When the temperature falls to about 60 °C, the sugar is kneaded with a machine to add many air bubbles till it turns white. ③ The 8 base colors are prepared and mixed to create various new colors, even darker or lighter tones by adjusting the ratio. ④ The whitened sugar is divided and colored accordingly. Pink is for Kintarou's face. Quick mixing is the key for an even color. ⑤ Before forming the shape, the colored sugar is cut into the right portions. This must be done before the sugar hardens and to keep all portions at an equal temperature. ⑥ Colored parts are layered on top of each other from the bottom. Then, a couple of skilled artisans roll the heavy candy block to shape it.

⑦初步成形后的金太郎饴糖直径有 30 厘米。以前没有的眼睫毛这样的细节，如今的师傅们也能很好地表现出来。一边平整形状一边导入糖坯辊压机，将糖坯拉成条状。

⑧将经过辊压机的糖放入另一台辊压机，使其粗细均匀。然后将条状的糖小心地放在切台上。

⑨将整合过的糖，配合着切台的长度平均地切割排放。

⑩将整齐排放好的条状的糖，保持形状，切成 30 厘米长的长段。在切口处撒上小麦粉和玉米淀粉混合的粉末。将刀放在切合部位，用木锤子敲打。如果冷却过度的话就没办法切开，因此需要师傅们快速地共同作业。

⑪然后要切成细段。师傅们伴随着轻快的敲打声有节奏地作业，这样的手艺，是经验培养出来的。

⑫一次做好的金太郎饴糖有 7000 颗。每一颗脸上的表情稍有不同，还是温热的。在一楼的店铺就可以买到金太郎饴糖。（横切，平袋装 378 日元起）

⑦ This candy block is 30 cm in diameter. Eyelashes are the new addition that it did not have before. Keeping the figure intact, it is rolled more to fit in the Batch Roller, which stretches the candy into a stick. ⑧ Candy is transferred to the second roller to even out the thickness. The candy connected like a rope is carefully pulled onto the board. ⑨ The candy in its final thickness is cut into the length of the board and lined up. ⑩ While maintaining its shape, neatly arranged candy is cut into 30 cm. Flour and corn starch mixture is dusted onto it. A knife is placed on the point to be cut and hit with a wooden stick. Artisans work together quickly before the candy gets too cold to cut. ⑪ Finally, it is cut into small pieces. The skillful artisans make a rhythmic sound. ⑫ From this batch, 7,000 pieces are made. Each face is unique and still warm. They are available on the 1st floor. (¥378 & up/ flat bag of cut candies)

KINTAROUAMEHONTEN

第三章

和果子的新浪潮

THE NEW WAVE OF WAGASHI

改写东京的和果子版图，
引领新潮流、值得瞩目的店铺

每日都会涌现新事物的东京，在饮食方面变化尤其迅速。而关于和果子，最值得关注的是年轻人开创的具有独立个性的店铺、成立设计事务所的和果子品牌以及大型和果子企业的新产线。以健康为导向，对选材要求严格、提倡自然平衡饮食理念的店铺，以及那些从和果子创意、点心包装到店铺装修风格都进行总体设计的和果子品牌等，他们的追求和讲究让人瞠目结舌。在本章中，让我们跟随《东京艺术之旅》编辑团队，探访一下从东京众多的新式和果子铺中精心挑选出来的店铺。

第三章

Latest trends that will redraw our Tokyo Wagashi Map
Don t miss out on these fascinating shops

Every day, new movements constantly appear and fade away in Tokyo. Particularly, the food industry changes rapidly. Regarding the wagashi world, what must be mentioned here are the unique stores independently opened by new generations, a new wagashi brand established by a design studio, or a new line of products introduced by a famous wagashi maker. It is quite fascinating to discover a wagashi shop that uses only selected healthy ingredients under a macrobiotic concept, or another shop designed entirely, not only wagashi products but also the packaging and even the interior, by their own hands. In this part, we will introduce our choice of the best new wagashi shops among lots of other information gathered by the "TOKYO ARTRIP" editors team.

ARTRIP ADVISER
艺术之旅顾问

TOKYO ARTRIP

《东京艺术之旅》编辑团队
Bijutsu Shuppan-sha
"TOKYO ARTRIP"
editors team

2017 年 10 月开始成立的系列丛书《东京艺术之旅》的编辑团队，从艺术到饮食，每日广泛收集最新的东京情报。

The editors team of the "TOKYO ARTRIP," series of books started in October 2017. Everyday, we gather a variety of information about Tokyo, from art to food.

⓰ HIGASHIYA man（南青山）

提倡将和果子的魅力融合于现今时代的 HIGASHIYA，从 2003 年在目黑川沿岸开业的一家小小的店铺做起，现在已经拥有南青山、银座两家门店。味道自不用说，无论是素材的搭配、尺寸大小，还是包装设计都走在新式和果子界的前沿。如今 HIGASHIYA man 迎来了创业十周年，已经融入了街景。馒头蒸笼里冒出的水蒸气会从店内飘散到街上，为表参道平添了一丝人情味。约 13 平方米大小的店铺里面，商品丰富多样。从店铺简洁的陈列摆设上，也可以隐约窥见日本的审美意识。

(时)11:00—19:00 (电) 03-5414-3881 (休)无 (址)港区南青山 3-17-14 (交)地铁千代田线、银座线、半藏门线表参道站步行 2 分钟 (网)www.higashiya.com/

⓰ HIGASHIYA man (MINAMI AOYAMA)

HIGASHIYA suggests the goodness of wagashi that matches a modern lifestyle. The shop has started from a small residential house by Meguro river since 2003, and now they have two locations in Minami Aoyama and Ginza. HIGASHIYA leads the new wagashi world, not to mention its taste, offering carefully determined combinations of ingredients, in suitably-sized, and impressive packaging. After over 10 years since their opening, HIGASHIYA man blends in the scenery of the town as if it has been there for decades. White steam from the manju steamer comes out of its window. The store is only 13m^2, yet they carry a good variety of sweets that would be perfect for gifts. The simple and beautiful display arrangement represents a Japanese sense of beauty.

(H)11:00-19:00 (T)03-5414-3881 (C)None (Ad)3-17-14 Minami Aoyama, Minato-ku (Ac)2-min. walk from Omotesando Station (Tokyo Metro Chiyoda Line, Ginza Line, Hanzoumon Line) (U)www.higashiya.com/

HIGASHIYA 最中

黑色纸盒上面只有和最中饼皮一样的浮雕花纹。里面装有条状的最中饼皮和袋装馅料，完全就像一套手工套件。墨色饼皮散发出浓郁的黑芝麻香气。让顾客可以动手打造自己的吃法，是如今新式和果子的流行趋势。能够和六种馅料完美搭配的饼皮也是精髓。（1 盒 2 份装，756 日元）

HIGASHIYA MONAKA

The noble black paper box has only a simple embossed pattern of monaka wafers. What you will find in the box are monaka wafer sticks and an paste in a pouch, just like a craft kit. These toasty black monaka wafers are put together with the rich and smooth black sesame *an* paste. Preparing your own sweets is the fun part of this new style of wagashi. Each of the 6 *an* flavors is paired with matching types of monaka wafers, selected in HIGASHIYA's stylish manner. (¥756/box of 2)

HIGASHIYA man

一口果子

传说和果子最初的形态就是用水果和坚果做成的一口大小的小点心。上图从近到远分别是桧枝、路考茶、深支子、紫根、鸟之子、枣，拥有日本传统颜色的和果子，寓意深刻。每一个风味各不相同，姿态小巧可爱。而如同画轴一样的包装，打开来倍增乐趣。（1盒6颗装，1944日元）

HITOKUCHIGASHI

Fruits and nuts, which are said to be the root of confectionery, are used for these bite-size sweets. Sweets in traditional colors have classy names: from the front, Hiwada, Rokoucha, Kokikuchinashi, Shikon, Torinoko, Natsume Butter. Each lovely ball uses a different flavored *an*. The scroll like packaging gives you a feeling of anticipation when unboxing. (¥1,944/box of 6 assorted flavors)

第三章

HIGASHIYA 米花糖

平安时代就有关于"米花糖"的相关记载。严格挑选的素材和散发着香气的干米组合起来，口感出色。干米就是煮熟或者蒸熟的米饭干燥后的米粒。这款"生姜"口味的米花糖，用生姜汁和南瓜子来调味，带着淡淡的辛辣感，十分清爽。其他还有"荞麦果实""大德寺纳豆"口味。（1罐20个装，1512日元）

HIGASHIYA OKOSHI

"Okoshi-gome," whose name has been known since about 1000 years ago, is the origin of "OKOSHI." This crunchy snack is made with selected ingredients and "*Hoshii*," which is dehydrated cooked rice. This "Ginger" flavored OKOSHI uses ginger juice and pumpkin seeds as an accent. It has the refreshing mild hotness. There are also "Soba-no-Mi "(Buckwheat) and "Daitokuji *Natto*"(fermented soy beans) flavors available. (¥1,512/can of 20 pcs)

HIGASHIYA man

和三盆豆

圆滚滚的可爱的小豆子点心。其发祥据说是在很早以前的平安、奈良时代，豆子作为和果子的原材料，其使用方法可谓多种多样。这款"和三盆豆"，是用甜味柔和的高级和三盆糖，裹着大颗的花生米做成。其他还有用白芝麻豆腐、竹炭、梅干等独具个性的素材做出来的八种不同口味。将色彩缤纷的小盒子组合起来，作为小礼物送人很合适。（1盒648日元）

WASANBONMAME

These cute little snacks are called *mamegashi* (a bite-sized cracker with beans or nuts inside). Their origin is believed to go back as far as 1000 years ago. Various wagashi commonly use beans in many ways. This "WASANBONMAME" has a large peanut coated with wasanbon sugar that adds an elegant mellow sweetness to it. Besides WASANBONMAME, mamegashi in various flavors using unique ingredients are available such as white sesame-tofu, bamboo charcoal, umeboshi (pickled plum), and so on. With your own creativity, mix and match the colorful boxes to make your personalized set of gifts. (¥648/box)

HIGASHIYA 煎饼

第一次拿到这个薄木盒的时候,忍不住猜测这里面到底是什么东西。里面装的是直径 9 厘米的薄煎饼。一片片用心烤制而成,入口嘎嘣酥脆。是一款让人怀念的、带着淡淡甜味的煎饼。两片一组的独立包装将美味很好地封存起来。保质期有 90 天,作为简单的伴手礼很受欢迎。(1 盒 8 片装,972 日元)

HIGASHIYA SENBEI

When you hold this box for the first time, it will make you wonder what is inside. It is made of paper-thin sheets of wood, called "Keiki-bako." These baked treats are about 9 cm in diameter with relief on the surface. Each piece is baked with care and has a light, airy texture. It is nostalgic, mildly sweet senbei. A set of two is packed individually. It is good for 90 days, so it will be a perfect gift for any occasion. (¥972/box of 8pcs)

HIGASHIYA man

⓱ 和果子 结（新宿）

店铺旨在做出能将人与人连接起来的和果子，超越时代，走向世界。创立 380 多年的和果子老店"两口屋是清"，在推广日本丰富的四季风情和传统的同时，挑战创新，创立了新品牌"结"。2016 年在东京成立的这家店铺，装修以白色为基调，具有简约现代风格。里面展示着色彩绚丽的和果子。这是师傅们长期以来不断追求和改进后，创造出的各式各样的和果子。一起来享受一下让人赏心悦目的"手心上的美"吧。

(时)8:00—22:00　(电)03-3353-5521　(休)无　(址)涩谷区千驮谷 5-24-55　NEWoMan 2 楼 ekinaka
(交)JR 新宿站步行 3 分钟　(网)www.wagashi-yui.tokyo/

⓱ WAGASHI YUI (SHINJUKU)

Provide wagashi that connects people together, throughout the ages, and beyond borders. A long-established wagashi shop with over 380 years of history, "Ryoguchiya Korekiyo," has started a new brand "YUI" to introduce innovative wagashi while cherishing seasonal beauty and tradition of Japan, which opened in 2016 in Tokyo. It employs a simple, modern taste interior design using white as its base color so that colorful wagashi stands out well. A lot of innovative wagashi have been created by the artisans with many years of experience in the world of wagashi. You cannot keep your eyes off these brilliant "palm-sized beauties."

(H) 8:00-22:00　(T) 03-3353-5521　(C) None　(Ad) NEWoMan 2nd Floor Ekinaka (within the station), 5-24-55 Sendagaya, Shibuya-ku　(Ac) 3-min. walk from Shinjuku Station (JR Line)　(U) www.wagashi-yui.tokyo/

第三章

干果子 珠珠

一颗颗用纸细心包起来的和三盆糖,白色和另一种颜色鲜艳的半球形糖果组成一对,将两个黏在一起,就成了一颗小圆珠,因而起名"珠珠"。红梅色、裏叶柳、藤黄等,都是日本自古以来传统的颜色名字。这款点心入口即化,只在舌尖留下梦幻般的香甜之味。三角形的包装很有个性。(1盒756日元,立方形2376日元)

HIGASHI JUJU

A pair of wasanbon sugar candies are carefully wrapped in a piece of paper. One candy is a white half-moon and the other is brightly colored. Combined, they make a small ball, called "JUJU." Traditional Japanese names of colors are used such as "Koubai-iro" (pink), "Uraha Yanagi" (green), "Touou" (yellow), and so on. A fleeting sweetness dissolves instantly in your mouth. The triangular packaging is another unique feature, too. (¥756/box, ¥2,376/cube box)

WAGASHI YUI

铜锣烧 圆满

糯糯的外皮,里面是分量十足的带皮红豆颗粒馅。这种保留完整颗粒熬制出来的馅料是日式传统的纯正味道。店铺的商标火印,是三个弧形的猴子图案。在日本,"弧猴"的图案象征着:如果人能够克制住自己心中的一个欲望,就能实现真实的愿望。(1 个 216 日元,6 个盒装 1512 日元)

DORAYAKI TSUBURAKA

The glutinous textured pancakes are generously filled with *tsubu-an*. The inherited tradition creates the authentic taste of *an* made without mashing beans. The store's logo imprinted on its surface is called "Mitsu-kukuri-saru" (literal translation is three bound monkeys). It is believed that your wish may be granted by sacrificing one of your desires. (¥216/pc, ¥1,512/box of 6)

第三章

干果子 招福

以秋天为主题，造型象征着欣赏中秋明月的可爱的兔子。这款以吉祥物为主题的和三盆糖，取材于身边的动植物和故事传说，精雕细琢，十分精美，是一款能够充分体现师傅们精巧手艺的华丽干果子。点心装在高级的杉木盒里，打开盖子，和三盆糖的香气迎面而来。"招福"和果子的主题通常根据四季更迭变换。作为礼物送人最合适。（杉木盒装 2160 日元）

HIGASHI MEDETAZUKUSHI

In this autumn-themed box, the red and white pretty bunnies are looking up at the beautiful harvest moon. MEDETAZUKUSHI is a box full of wasanbon sugar candies featuring lucky charms. They are delicately shaped into familiar animals, plants or stories. These delightful higashi are derived from the exceptional technique of artisans. An elegant cedar box is used for the packaging, so when you open the lid, the natural scent comes out of the box along with the seasonally-designed higashi. This is the perfect gift for a special occasion. (¥2,160/cedar box assort)

WAGASHI YUI

⓲ 和果子工坊 丝（东十条）

"丝可以编成绳子、布匹，以及人与人之间的纽带。"这家店铺的主人，从小就对日本传统文化很有兴趣，选择了制作和果子的道路。店主在开店前两年接受订制和果子并参与不定期活动，2015年如愿开了店铺。放置在和式古董器具上的和果子，有店主出生地宫崎特产的"芝士馒头""酸橘饼""干琥珀""一口最中"等带着温暖气息的小巧的手工点心。每月只营业3天。因为营业时间有限，去之前要先在网页上查询清楚。

(时) 12:00—14:00 每月3天 (电) 无 (休) 不固定 (址) 北区中十条1-10-1 (交) JR十条站或京滨东北线东十条站步行7分钟 (网) www.ito-wagashi.com

⓲ WAGASHIKOBO ITO ito (HIGASHI JUJO)

"A thread becomes a woven string and a woven cloth for wrapping around things. Then eventually, it connects people." The owner of this shop had a keen interest in traditional Japanese culture as a child, which led her to be a wagashi pâtissière as she is today. She had been accepting custom order requests and participated in occasional events for two years before she opened her dream shop in 2015. The heart-warming handmade small wagashi displayed on antique Japanese fixtures include the specialties of her hometown, Miyazaki Prefecture, "Cheese-man" and "Hebesu" (a type of citrus)-mochi, and other pretty treats such as "Hoshi *Kohaku*"(made with agar and arrowroot flour), or "Hitokuchi Monaka." The shop opens only for limited hours, three times a month, so be sure to check her website for the next business day.

(H) 12:00-14:00 Open three days a month (T) None (C) Occasional (Ad) 1-10-1 Nakajujo, Kita-ku (Ac) 7-min. walk from Jujo Station (JR Line) / Higashi Jujo Station (JR Keihin Touhoku Line) (U) www.ito-wagashi.com/

第三章

你们在哪里啊

一款光看点心名,就让人十分怀念的上果子。这是半订制的点心,以小孩子们玩耍手拍线球的场景为灵感设计制作,是一款使用让人放心的高品质日本本土红小豆熬制的馅料做成的练切点心。绚丽的色彩,是用天然素材着色而成。伴手礼包装需要另外付费,未经漂白的粗布料包裹着点心盒,怀旧感十足。(1个300日元起,需提前1个月预约)

ANTAGATADOKOSA

A *jogashi* (higher quality fresh wagashi) with a name that would probably make you feel nostalgic. This is semi order-made with a design motif of an embroidered hand ball which Japanese girls used to play with. A ball of smooth *an* made with quality and trusted Japanese red beans is inside this nerikiri. It is beautifully colored with only natural ingredients. Gift wrapping using unbleached cloth is available for an additional fee. The result is compellingly heart-warming. (¥300/pc, order taken 1 month in advance)

WAGASHIKOBO ITO ito

⑲ 竹野和萩饼（樱新町）

店内极小的空间里面，样品摆放得整整齐齐。这家店于 2016 年开业，极大地改变了一直以来用糯米和豆沙馅制作萩饼的理念。店主从小就非常喜欢奶奶做的萩饼，他想把这份美味和大家一起分享，带着这样的想法开了这家店铺，店名把奶奶的名字"竹野"也加了进去。出品只有两种豆沙馅的基础萩饼和五种每日点心套装。每日点心套装目前已经有一百多种。这些精心挑选过的食材做成的萩饼给食客带来视觉和味觉的双重享受，这正是和果子的新风潮。

⑰12:00—18:00（售完即止） ⑰ 03-6413-1227 ⑰星期一、星期二 ⑰世田谷区樱新町 1-21-1
⑰东急田园都市线樱新町站步行 4 分钟 ⑰无

⑲ TAKENO TO OHAGI (SAKURASHINMACHI)

This minimalistic specialty shop neatly displays samples of *ohagi* (sweet glutinous rice balls). Glutinous rice and *an* are the standard ingredients for ohagi, but these norms are being changed here since 2016. The owner grew up loving his grandma's ohagi. Naming the shop after the grandma Takeno, the owner hopes to share her tasty ohagi with many customers. The menu includes two different kinds of *an* as basic items, as well as five specials of the day. More than 100 flavors have been created so far. With carefully selected ingredients, this new wave of ohagi would surely catch your eye while entertaining your taste buds.

(H) 12:00-18:00 (close when sold out) (T) 03-6413-1227 (C) Mondays and Tuesdays (Ad) 1-21-11 Sakurashinmachi, Setagaya-ku (Ac) 4-min. walk from Sakurashinmachi Station (Tokyu Den-en Toshi Line) (U) N/A

每日萩饼套装

将煮好的糯米团成团,用不同馅料和原料将小小的糯米团做成各种可爱的造型。萩饼的传统内馅是清甜的白豆沙,但这家店在材料上做了很多创新尝试,让人惊喜不已。图中最下方的萩饼是炙烤玉米口味,将炭烤过的香甜玉米粒和白豆沙混合在一起做成内馅。顺时针方向分别为混合4种坚果口味的萩饼,斑纹状、以抹茶和艾草为原料的清新口味萩饼,杧果内馅加上椰丝的原创水果口味的萩饼以及李子酱和白豆沙混合制成的萩饼。(单个180—280日元)

OHAGI

Glutinous rice balls are carefully formed not to mash grains. Portraying these rice balls as small canvases, they skillfully place *an* and other ingredients on top as if to complete art work. Oo-tebo kidney beans are used for moderately-sweetened *shiro-an* (white *an*), which is the main ingredient of the coating. Clockwise from the front: Roasted Corn (grilled *an* with roasted-corn); Nuts (4 types of pesticides-free nuts); Green Tea with Mugwort (sweet and bitter *an*'s making spiral); Mango and Organic Coconut; Plum (pureed plum and shiro-*an*). (from ¥180 to ¥280/pc)

TAKENO TO OHAGI

⓴ 厨点心黑木（本乡）

"厨"字意味着师傅们的手工制作。这里是日本料理店黑木开设的日式风格时尚咖啡馆姊妹店。店铺的理念是每日将新鲜出炉的和果子在最好的状态下提供给客人，让客人可以调动五感全身心来感受这真正的美味。店铺旨在促使传统和果子文化的推广，为和果子的发展做贡献。精美新鲜的和果子，搭配猿田彦咖啡。由建筑家隈研吾操刀设计的这家店铺，位于东京大学本乡校园内。这是一个能够一边品尝和果子，一边享受最美妙的休闲时间的好地方。

⊙ 9:00—19:00 ⓔ 03-5802-5577 ⓗ 特定休假（跟随东京大学） ⓐ 文京区本乡 7-3-1 东京大学本乡校园春日门旁边，大和学术研究馆 1 楼 ⓒ 地铁丸之内线本乡 3 丁目站步行 5 分钟或都营地铁大江户线本乡 3 丁目站步行 4 分钟 ⓝ www.wagashi-kurogi.co.jp

⓴ KURIYA KASHI KUROGI (HONGO)

Kuriya means artisan's works. KUROGI is a modern, Japanese style café by a chef from a popular high-class Japanese restaurant, Kurogi. It aims to serve freshly prepared wagashi at their best and to let all the sensations be stimulated by real sweets. The chef has set out to take traditional wagashi to a new level to contribute to the development of wagashi. Beautiful and fresh wagashi served with popular Sarutahiko coffee. Designed by distinguished architect, Kengo Kuma, this café is situated in Tokyo University (Hongo campus). The best location to enjoy blissful moments with wagashi.

(H) 9:00-19:00 (T) 03-5802-5577 (C) Holidays dependent on the university schedule (Ad) 1st Floor, Daiwa Ubiquitous Research Building, 7-3-1, Hongo, Bunkyo-ku (located nearby the Kasuga Gate inside Hongo campus of The University of Tokyo) (Ac) 5-min. walk from Hongo 3-chome Station (Tokyo Metro Marunouchi Line) / 4-min. walk from Hongo 3-chome Station (Toei-Oedo Line) (U) www.wagashi-kurogi.co.jp/

第三章

干果子

外盒包装使用的是以店铺商标为创意的黑白现代感设计。选用德岛生产的高纯度和三盆制作的"和三盆糖"。造型采用商标图案，颜色粉嫩，颇有格调。点心入口即化。盒子和点心还有其他不同款的设计种类可供选择，也可以带回家自己一人享受这份高级的味蕾体验。（1盒1080日元）

HIGASHI

Packaged in a modern design featuring the café logo in black and white, HIGASHI, wasanbon candy is crafted using only high quality wasanbon sugar harvested in Tokushima Prefecture. The café's logo is also reproduced in the sweets in classy pastel colors. It crumbles and melts in your mouth. As there are different types of packaging or designs of the sweet, you can get a takeout and enjoy the atmosphere of the café at home. (¥1,080/box)

KURIYA KASHI KUROGI　　　　　　　　　　91

蕨饼 mayura

原本只是店内堂食的蕨饼,竟发展出可以在家里品尝的高级版本。有"黑蜜"和"抹茶"两种口味。蕨饼被装在高级的桐木盒子里面。食用前,撒上附带的黄豆粉、青豆粉和抹茶的混合调味粉。食材使用珍贵的蕨粉,柔软有弹力,甜味和芳香之气完美交融。(预约优先,1盒4 000日元)

WARABIMOCHI MAYURA

This was developed for customers to enjoy the café specialty at home. Luxuriously presented in an exclusive paulownia wood box are two types of *warabimochi* (bracken starch dumpling) with muscovado syrup and green tea. Before eating, coat them with the powdered soybean and/or the mixture of powdered green soybean and green tea. As this warabimochi is made with rare pure bracken root starch, you will enjoy the marriage of a gently chewy texture with a nutty ground-bean flavor. (Advance orders preferred. ¥4,000/box)

㉑ 和果子 巡（代代木上原）

巡的店主说他们只售卖香甜可爱、能愉悦身心的美味和果子。这些将自然平衡饮食与和果子完美融合而诞生的点心，只选取自然栽培和有机栽培的安全食材。里面的砂糖、小麦粉、鸡蛋、乳制品，全部没有使用任何添加剂。如今这些对健康和美容有益的点心在日本十分受欢迎。各种食材巧妙结合，甜料仅使用不会导致血糖值上升的有机龙舌兰糖浆。这个崭新的创意是店主黑岩典子基于"做自己想吃的和果子"这个理念。在店铺里慢慢品尝时令生果子，原料豆子和调味粉也在店中售卖，不可错过。

时 10:30—18:00 电 03-5738-8050 休 星期一 址 涩谷区上原 3-2-1 交 小田急线或地铁千代田线代代木上原站步行 5 分钟 网 www.wa-meguri.com/

第三章

㉑ WANOKASHI MEGURI（YOYOGIUEHARA）

Sweets with a delightful look and taste that your body would be grateful for were developed by fusing macrobiotic ingredients and wagashi-making. Natural or organic ingredients are selected, with no use of sugar, wheat, eggs, dairy, or additives. Health and beauty benefits are much appreciated. "Making sweets that I want to eat" is the ethos behind the creation of skillfully devised recipes by the owner, Noriko Kuroiwa. Only low GI organic agave syrup is used as a sweetener. Relax and enjoy wagashi with fresh and seasonal ingredients. Beans and flour they use are available to purchase at the café.

(H)10:30-18:00 (T)03-5738-8050 (C)Mondays (Ad)3-2-1, Uehara, Shibuya-ku (Ac)5-min. walk from Yoyogi-uehara Station (Odakyu Line, Tokyo Metro Chiyoda Line) (U)www.wa-meguri.com/

杂粮豆大福 巡福

"大福的'福',幸福的'福',给食用的人带来的福气,会随着体内血液一起循环。"这款基础商品蕴含了这样一个美好的愿望。用糙糯米、藜麦制成的饼皮中还有黑豆,里面是手工精心制作的馅料。馅料原材料是小豆和不会引起血糖值上升的龙舌兰糖浆。略带颗粒感的红豆馅搭配柔软的外皮,口感十分美妙。每周末,还有一款限定口味。(1个378日元)

ZAKKOKUMAMEDAIFUKU FUKUMEGURI

Fuku in DAIFUKU means fortune. This signature sweet was created "wishing the fortune circulates among people, as the healthy blood circulates in their bodies." Plump black soybeans are in the brown glutinous rice and quinoa mochi. Inside is hand-made *an* made with red beans and agave syrup for the prevention of a blood sugar spike. Choose from moderately-sweetened *tsubu-an* or unsieved smooth *an* with the benefit of whole red beans. Another special filling is available on weekends only. (¥378/pc)

第三章

笑逐颜开馅

EMIKOBORERU-AN

一眼看去，好像松露一样的这款点心，里面是生巧克力内馅，是一款带有不同感觉的和果子。馅料有使用独特材料制作出来的"柔滑馅料""白色软馅""抹茶馅""南瓜馅"四种。内馅和上面的椰丝十分相配，放入口中，好吃到让人忍不住微笑。这款带着橘味利口酒香的成熟味道的和果子，很适合平时不爱甜点的人。（1 个 324 日元，4 种盒装 1296 日元）

At first glance, you might think they are Japanese style chocolate truffles. In fact, ganache wrapped in *an*, is a new sensation of wagashi. Prepared with four flavors of *an* with unique ingredients; smooth, white smooth, green tea and pumpkin. The desiccated coconut coating is a perfect match; so delectable that you cannot help smiling with the first bite you take. The sophisticated taste with Cointreau is appreciated by those who cannot handle too much sweetness. (¥324/pc, ¥1,296/box of 4)

しろいくろ

白黒

执着于黑与白
精心设计的特别讲究的店铺与和果子

Designed the shop in black and white
Putting thought into the confectionery in black and white

❷❷ 白黑（麻布十番）

伫立在商业街的小巷子里，像一座古老民居一样的店铺。店主是一位美术设计师兼建筑师，他充分发挥自己职业特长，在 2012 年创立了这家店铺。点心的主题和店名"白黑"相呼应，统一采用白色和黑色。店铺的茶点菜单，除了用最高级的丹波黑豆做的咸豆大福之外，还有五种点心、黑豆茶及咖啡。整条街道洋溢着一种怀旧的气氛，但许多新文化的种子在这里被孕育。

(时)10:00—18:00 (电)03-3454-7225 (休)不固定 (址)港区麻布十番 2-8-1 (交)地铁南北线或都营地铁大江户线麻布十番站步行 4 分钟 (网)shiroikuro.com

❷❷ SHIROIKURO（AZABUJYUBAN）

At a back alley of a busy street is this traditional-home-turned-into café, opened by two talented people, a graphic designer and an architect in 2012. To match the house name "SHIROIKURO" (White black), theme colors of the sweets are also black and white. The café offers Salted-Black-Soybean Daifuku with the top quality Tamba black soybean; five other sweets; and black-soybean tea or coffee. The atmosphere that embodies the saying, "Today is yesterday's pupil" blends well with this town.

(H)10:00-18:00 (T)03-3454-7225 (C)Occasional (Ad)2-8-1 Azabujuban, Minato-ku (Ac)4-min. walk from Azabujuban Station (Tokyo Metro Namboku Line, Toei-Ooedo Line) (U)shiroikuro.com

SHIROIKURO

① "甜咸"风味、甜味比较淡的咸豆大福。小仓带皮红豆馅、黑豆和麻糬饼这几种不同的美味，完美地融合在一款点心中，堪称极品。点心形状小巧，极为优雅。(1个259日元，黑豆茶270日元)
② 外带用的正方形的盒子，统一采用简约现代风格。(6个装1555日元)

① Salted-Black-Soybean Daifuku, moderately sweetened as the owner strived to achieve the salty-sweetness. Ogura-an, black-soybeans and mochi. These three elements are combined to create an unrivalled taste. The elegantly small daifuku makes you feel that you could have another one. (¥259/pc; Black Soybean Tea ¥270).
② The design of the square gift box is simple yet modern. (¥1,555/box of 6)

第三章

③黑豆咸味瑞士卷，分为"白卷"和"黑卷"。白卷里面的馅料是黑豆鲜奶油，外层是柠檬风味的海绵蛋糕。黑卷的外层是竹炭和黑可可风味的蛋糕卷，里面是特制的浓郁芝士奶油。(1块356日元，1整条1620日元)
④摆放在复古风格的橱窗里的巧克力蛋糕也是热门商品。可可豆的苦涩和黑豆的甘甜融为一体，散发出阵阵香气。(1块259日元)

③ "White" and "Black", salted swiss rolls with black soybeans. "White", lemon flavored white sponge with black soybeans in fresh cream. "Black", refreshing bamboo charcoal and black cocoa sponge with special cream cheese. (¥356/slice, ¥1,620/whole) ④ Inside this retro box is another popular sweet, Gateau au Chocolat. Harmony between the bitterness of cacao and the sweetness of black soybean comes with a delightful aroma. (¥259/pc)

SHIROIKURO

和果子与日本茶，女店主一个人的舞台
WAGASHI AND TEA. TEA MASTER'S ONE-WOMAN SHOW

茶室"点心屋九道"里面，提供一份历时约两个小时的茶道茶点体验套餐，包含七碟点心及与之相配的茶饮。主持这个套餐的是业界顶尖的和果子艺术家沟口实穗。从小就喜欢和果子，对和果子有很深研究的她，推崇符合当今时代的和果子。在节奏匆忙的日常生活中，抽出一点时间，在茶室里与自我对话，这也正是茶道的精神。品尝这些和果子，认真咀嚼，在享受美味的同时，可以静静地思考，让自己沉静下来。在这样非日常的地方，充分调动自己的五感，这也将成为一次难忘的经历。

Saryo KASHIYA KOKONOTSU offers a two-hour tea session with seven dishes of wagashi and accompanying cups of tea. A conscientious wagashi artist, Miho Mizoguchi, who grew up appreciating wagashi offers contemporary wagashi with traditional cultural bases. Being silent during the tea-serving session, escaping daily business, means facing yourself. You would then notice the simple things in life such as to take time when enjoying sweets, or to chew well when eating. Detach yourself from routines and use all five senses. It will be an experience to remember.

点心屋九道（御徒町）

(时)预约制 (电)无 (休)不固定 (址)台东区鸟越 1-32-2 (交)JR 御徒町站步行 13 分钟 (网) kokonotsu-9.jugem.jp

KASHIYA-KOKONOTSU（OKACHIMACHI）

(H)Reservation only (T)N/A (C)Occasional (Ad)1-32-2 Torigoe, Taito-ku (Ac)13-min. walk from Okachimachi Station (JR Line) (U)kokonotsu-9.jugem.jp

第三章

房间是以黑色为基调的复古风格，里面播放着优雅的钢琴曲，让人很放松。这份历时两小时的茶点套餐中提供的配茶种类有煎茶、红茶、焙茶、台湾茶等。里面也有一些店主在旅行时发现的珍贵稀少的地方茶。整个冲泡的过程十分优美。

In the two-hour-session sitting in the retro jet-black interior with soft piano music, to go with wagashi, several cups of tea are served: green, black, roasted green, Taiwanese as well as rare teas personally found overseas. Ms. Mizoguchi's sophisticated demeanour and beautiful form when making tea is impressive.

盘中的艺术：精致的器皿上盛放着看似朴素却又极具艺术感的和果子。套餐中的 7 盘和果子包括咸甜口味的和果子，不喜欢甜食的客人也可以尝试一下这个套餐。茶室中摆放和提供的器具都是店主从名匠手中订制或挑选而来的。店内同时贩卖一些名家的精美和式器具作品。

A piece of art: Minimal but unique wagashi made with choice ingredients served on exclusive tableware. Seven dishes include some savory. Each piece of crockery is made to order by artists. Tea ceramics and accessories of "20 KOKONOTSU Selection" are available for purchase.

101

第四章

平民街的和果子

WAGASHI IN DOWNTOWN TOKYO

优哉游哉享用平民和果子，
可以和朋友一起分享的美味

出生于马喰町、在浅草桥长大的松野弘，是把落语当作兴趣的土生土长的江户人。"我从小就生活在平民街，提到和果子，我能想起的，就是可以随意拿在手里吃的好吃的和果子。"据他说，在学生时代，他曾经在浅草寺商业街的人形烧店铺"木村家总店"（见 107 页）做过兼职。现在他还不时会买一些鲷鱼烧和铜锣烧带回工作间当零食。"必须是好吃的，而且可以放轻松吃的和果子。"他说，和大家一起分享的话会觉得很开心，气氛也会变得很融洽。

第四章

Take it easy with wagashi from Downtown Tokyo
A happy moment with your friends and family

A genuine Tokyoite, Hiroshi Matsuno was born in Bakuro-cho, grew up in Asakusa-bashi, and loves Rakugo (traditional comic storytelling) . "I have always lived in this region. As for wagashi, the ones from local shops are the best. You can enjoy them casually, by eating with your hands." Matsuno told us that, as a university student, he used to work for KIMURAYA HONTEN (see P107) that sells ningyoyaki (doll-shaped cake with filling of *an*) in Nakamise shopping street next to Sensoji Temple. Now he often takes some taiyaki (fish-shaped cake with filling of *an*) and dorayaki to his work as refreshments for his employees. For Matsuo, wagashi must be "delicious and easy to eat without fuss." Good wagashi would make us all smile, he said.

ARTRIP ADVISER
艺术之旅顾问

松野弘
Hiroshi Matsuno

创业于 1945 年，是位于马喰町的"生活器具松野屋"的第三代店主。店铺原本是一家箱包批发店，现在成了一家经营以自然材料为中心的生活器具的杂货店，很受欢迎。著作有《杂货图鉴》（蜻蜓书系列，新潮社出版）。

He is the third generation of Matsunoya (est.1945) dealing household tools in Bakuro-cho. Started as a bag wholesaler, Matsunoya is now a popular wholesaler of utensils made with naturally derived materials. Matsuno wrote *Aramono Zukan* (Encyclopedia of Household Tools) (Tombo-no-hon series, Shinchosha Publishing).

浅草寺商业街
人形烧店铺

来自世界各国的游客让商业街变得十分繁荣,永远充满活力。大排档风格的店铺一间挨着一间,热闹氛围当中,最有人气的东西应该是著名的人形烧吧。在这里发祥壮大的人形烧,已经成了浅草寺的名物。出炉时趁热食用,或者带回去当伴手礼都很好。把这里的五家人形烧店铺都尝一遍吧。

SENSOU-JI NAKAMISE

Crowded with visitors from around the world, Nakamise shopping street has always been a hive of activity- shops after shops, people after people. The star in this excitement is the local specialty, ningyoyaki. Born and bred in this region, ningyoyaki traditionally depicts icons around Sensoji Temple. Served fresh from the oven or cold as a take-home souvenir. Let's visit five different ningyoyaki shops here in Nakamise.

木村家总店

浅草寺的象征
人形烧历史开始的地方

Depicting Icons of Sensoji Temple
The History of Ningyoyaki Started Here

㉓ 木村家总店（浅草）

固定的地址，不变的味道。离浅草寺寺院最近的是从1868年开始在商业街经营人形烧的店铺"木村家总店"。第一代店主设计的作为参拜浅草寺的象征造型的人形烧有五重塔、雷神、灯笼、鸽子四种。店铺里摆放着一台可以烤制四种形状的模具，由师傅们熟练轻巧地操作。制作一个人形烧所花费的时间约为3分20秒。据说一天大概可以烤2400个。有无馅和带馅两种。限量抹茶馅绝对不可错过。（4个带馅袋装300日元起，10个带馅盒装800日元起）

⑬ 9:00—19:00　⑪ 03-3841-7055　㈤ 不固定　㈥ 台东区浅草2-3-1　㊋ 地铁银座线或都营地铁浅草线浅草站步行5分钟　㉘ www.kimura-ya.co.jp

第四章

㉓ KIMURAYAHONTEN (ASAKUSA)

The same place and the same taste. Right next to the Sensoji Main Hall, is the first ningyoyaki shop opened on Nakamise in 1868, the original KIMURAYA HONTEN. The four shapes; Five-storied pagoda, Thunder God, Lantern and Dove, were created by the founder as the symbols of pilgrimage to Sensoji Temple. Behind the shop window are craftsmen baking the ningyoyaki using molds of four shapes. It takes 3 minutes 20 seconds to bake one batch. They bake 2,400 a day. Choose from with or without *an*. Try the limited green tea flavor, too. (¥300 & up/4pcs with an, or ¥800 & up/box of 10 with an)

(H) 9:00-19:00　(T) 03-3841-7055　(C) Occasional　(Ad) 2-3-1, Asakusa, Taito-ku　(Ac) 5-min. walk from Asakusa Station (Tokyo Metro Ginza Line, Toei-Asakusa Line)　(U) www.kimura-ya.co.jp/

KIMURAYAHONTEN　　　　　　　　　　　　　　　　　　　　　　　　　107

人形烧的售卖方法和包装各式各样，享受其中各不相同的乐趣

鸽子标识的木村家人形烧总店

位于仲见世商业街中间地段，鸽子的商标引人注目。人形烧的造型使用浅草寺的四种象征，有着和蛋糕一样松软的饼皮及独具风味的馅料。包装纸上的鸽子形象十分可爱，让人情不自禁停下脚步入店购买。

HATONOMARKU NO KIMURAYA NINGYOUYAKI HONPO

Halfway through Nakamise shopping street, is this shop with a big Hato (dove) logo. Their ningyoyaki is in four shapes that symbolize Sensoji, with its sponge cake-like fluffy pastry and flavorsome *an*. The images of doves printed on the packages on display are too cute to miss.

梅林堂 总店

位于雷门附近的梅林堂。亲切的氛围，从店门口不时传来中气十足的叫卖声。"1 个 50 日元"，非常便宜，新鲜出炉的人形烧买到手还是热乎乎的。10 个装只需要 500 日元。对于人形烧爱好者们来说，梅林堂的价格很划算。

HONKE BAIRINDOU

Right after the Kaminari-mon Gate, BAIRINDOU catches your eyes. A light-hearted atmosphere like a street stall, with lively chanting of the shopkeepers to call in customers. Fresh from the oven, ¥50/pc, baked fresh in the shop. ¥500/2 x bags of 10. A good buy for ningyoyaki lovers.

Different Trade Styles and Packaging. Enjoy the Difference

三鸠堂

店面布置十分简洁，三鸠堂位于商业街中间一带。手工烤制的豆沙馅人形烧有真空包装，可以买来当伴手礼。因为可以保存 1 个月，很受各国游客欢迎。每日会有定时打折促销活动，不容错过。

MIHATODOU

A simple interior of unvarnished wood makes this shop look neat and tidy. It is located about halfway down the Nakamise street. Hand-baked cakes with smooth *an*, which also come in vacuum-sealed bags that stay fresh for a month. Generous reduction in prices at "happy hour."

第四章

龟屋

传统的昭和风格店铺结构，售卖六种使用高级食材制作的人形烧。专心致志操作着模具的师傅们，吸引了很多游人驻足观看。龟屋的人形烧放上一天更加滋润好吃。

KAMEYA

A traditional shopfront that exudes old Japanese charm, KAMEYA offers ningyoyaki with quality ingredients in six shapes. The way the artisan earnestly bakes them using his beloved molds attracts the eyes of passers-by. The crispy skin settles the following day and tastes even better.

㉔ 清寿轩（人形町）

创业于 1861 年，在江户时代就颇有人气的和果子老铺。继承了第一代店主创造的味道和技术，如今已经到了第七代。经营品类有羊羹、栗子馒头和最中等。昭和初期开始售卖的"铜锣烧"，是这家店铺的招牌产品。总被预约售罄的大号烧和小号烧，吸引了无数食客。为了让每位客人都能体会到"初食"的感动，店铺坚守着上一代"绝对不松懈"的教诲，依然执着于传统的手工制作。另一家新店铺同时设有工厂，保留了江户情调，让人想要沉浸其中。

⸨时⸩9:00—17:00，周六 9:00—12:00（售完即止）⸨电⸩03-3661-0940 ⸨休⸩星期日、节假日 ⸨址⸩中央区日本桥堀留町 1-4-16 P-cosu 日本桥大楼 1 楼 ⸨交⸩地铁日比谷线或都营地铁浅草线人形町站步行 3 分钟，地铁银座线或半藏门线三越前站步行 6 分钟 ⸨网⸩seijuken.com

㉔ SEIJUKEN（NINGYOCHOU）

Historic confectioner established in 1861 (Edo-Period). Finesse to achieve the good taste has been passed on to the current seventh generation owner. Along with yokan and chestnut-manju, they have the signature dorayaki circa 1920's. Pre-order is essential for "Oban-yaki" and "Koban-yaki" (large/small dorayaki). They are high in demand among many repeating customers. The owner faithfully follows the ethos of his father: "Live up to the expectations of the delighted customers. Do not cut corners." The tradition of hand-made confectionery is maintained. The new premises with the atmosphere of Edo-era Japan has a factory attached.

(H) 9:00-17:00, Sat 9:00-12:00 (closed when sold out) (T) 03-3661-0940 (C) Sundays, Public Holidays (Ad) 1st Floor P-cosu Nihonbashi Building, 1-4-16 Nihonbashi Horidome-cho, Chuo-ku (Ac) 3-min. walk from Ningyocho Station (Tokyo Metro Hibiya Line, Toei-Asakusa Line) /6-min. walk from Mitsukoshi-mae Station (Tokyo Metro Ginza Line, Hanzoumon Line) (U) seijuken.com/

第四章

大判铜锣烧

松软饱满的饼皮里面，是光泽油亮的带皮豆馅。连饼皮都可以尽情品尝的大判铜锣烧直径有 10 厘米。保留着颗粒感的红豆馅，是在铜制的大锅里熬制 6 个小时，加入砂糖一起做成的。这个馅料和带着淡淡蜂蜜香味的饼皮十分搭配，口味一流。印着墨色文字的包装袋，令人印象深刻。从 2 个装到 16 个装，提供不同尺寸的包装。（1 个 220 日元）

DORAYAKI

Fluffy cake filled with shiny *tsubu-an*. Coming in a generous size of 10cm, you can enjoy every bit of it. To make tasty *an* with beautiful grains, slow cook red beans in a copper pot for six hours and add sugar at the end, then mix by hand. Their *an* and honey-flavored pancakes harmonize perfectly. Packaging has impressive brush writing of Daifuku-cho (an old merchants' accounting book meaning fortune). Choose from a pack of 2 up to 16. (¥220/pc)

SEIJUKEN

㉕ 浪花家总店（两国）

师傅们不停操作着长长的烧制模具，具有节奏感的咚咚声在店铺内回响。这家店"二战"前创业于银座，现在转移到两国的鲷鱼烧专卖店。创始人是跟着麻布十番的鲷鱼烧专卖店老板的师傅学习的弟子，现在的店主是第三代传人。一天烤制100至200个，不仅受到当地人的喜爱，从远方寻访过来的客人也很多。店内有堂食专区，还提供炒荞麦面和炒乌冬面等简餐，菜单很丰富。点两个鲷鱼烧就可以在店内食用，务必尝试一下新鲜出炉的热乎乎的美味。

(时)10:30—17:30，星期六、节假日 10:30—16:00 (电)03-3623-2667 (休)星期日，每月第2和第4个星期一，节假日第二天 (址)墨田区龟泽1-24-2 (交)都营地铁大江户线或JR两国站无需步行 (网)无

㉕ NANIWAYAHONTEN (RYOGOKU)

Rhythmical clanging noise of long-handled molds of a tai (snapper) echoes in the shop. This historical taiyaki shop started before WW II in Ginza, then moved to Ryogoku. The founder learned from a master chef who had trained the founder of the Azabu-Juban shop earlier. The current owner is the third generation. 100-200 pieces are baked a day and locals and visitors from faraway love them. Tables are available to enjoy taiyaki as well as varieties of light meals such as noodles. There is a minimum order of two to stay. Oven-fresh is the best.

(H)10:30-17:30, Sat & public holiday 10:30-16:00 (T)03-3623-2667 (C)Sundays, 2nd and 4th Mondays, any day after public holidays (Ad)1-24-2 Kamezawa, Sumida-ku (Ac)Less than 1 min. walk from Ryogoku Station (Toei-Ooedo Line, JR Line) (U)N/A

第四章

鲷鱼烧

这款鲷鱼烧连尾巴都被美味的红豆馅料塞得满满当当。基本上看不到烤焦的地方，白色的薄饼皮是它的特征。鲷鱼烧美味的秘密就在于店家的烤制火候和红豆馅的配方。大小很合适，女性也可以拿在手里吃。外带回家后用烤箱或者微波炉加热一下，就可以还原本的味道。（1个150日元）

TAIYAKI

Homemade *an*, made with beans harvested in Hokkaido, is stuffed from head to tail of this taiyaki. Thin pastry with a uniquely pale color, carefully baked not to burn. The secret is in the special ratio of ingredients and the baking expertise. A nice size for everyone. At home, warm up in the microwave oven or toaster oven and the original flavor will return. (¥150/pc)

NANIWAYAHONTEN

㉖ 舟和雷门店（浅草）

提到"番薯羊羹"，人们一定会想到舟和这家店。多年屹立不倒的著名品牌——舟和是一家位于浅草的老铺，从创业到现在已经经营了一百多年。开创者原本是番薯批发商，他从价格昂贵的炼羊羹中获得灵感，想要制作出"平民食用的羊羹"，于是与和果子师傅一起开创了这家店铺。如今发展壮大，包括提供茶饮的店铺，在浅草已经拥有七家分店。带馅团子和蒸栗子羊羹也很受欢迎。店铺意在给当地人以及来浅草旅游的人们提供新鲜出炉的产品。正是这一份决心，使其成为这条鲜活的街道中不可或缺的一家著名店铺。

(时) 10:00—19:00，星期六 9:30—20:00，星期日、节假日 9:30—19:30　(电) 03-5828-2701　(休) 无
(址) 台东区浅草 1-3-5　(交) 地铁银座线或都营地铁浅草线或东武伊势崎线浅草站步行 3 分钟
(网) funawa.jp/

㉖ FUNAWA KAMINARIMON（ASAKUSA）

As for *imoyokan* (sweet potato cake), FUNAWA has the quality that is next to none. It is a well-known imoyokan confectioner with a history of over 100 years in Asakusa. The founder, a sweet potato wholesaler, created this with a wagashi artisan as a "people's yokan," inspired by then expensive red-bean yokan. Funawa operates seven shops (café included) in Asakusa only. Anko-dama (an ball in firm jelly) and kuri-mushi-yokan (red-bean/chestnut steamed cake) are also popular. Funawa's love for Asakusa and spirit to offer the freshest ones to the customers made imoyokan a must-eat in this lively town.

(H) Mon-Fri 10:00-19:00, Sat 9:30-20:00, Sun and public holiday 9:30-19:30　(T) 03-5828-2701
(C) None　(Ad) 1-3-5 Asakusa, Taito-ku　(Ac) 3-min. walk from Asakusa Station (Tokyo Metro Ginza Line, Toei-Asakusa Line, Tobu-Isezaki Line)　(U) funawa.jp/

第四章

番薯羊羹

鲜艳的金黄色的羊羹,切成方便食用的大小,一个一个摆放在盒子里。为了保留食材原本的风味,原材料的白薯,连去皮都是手工操作完成。完全没有使用色素、保鲜剂、香料等,保质期只有三天。吃剩的羊羹,可以用烤箱烤一下,或者冷冻后食用。(5 条盒装 648 日元起)

IMOYOKAN

Bright golden yellow imoyokan packed in bite-size pieces in a gift box. Sweet potatoes are hand-peeled keeping their natural texture and flavor. Free from artificial coloring, preservatives and fragrances. Best consumed within 3 days of production. Any leftover can be warmed up in the oven or frozen to make an ice candy. (¥648/box of 5)

FUNAWA KAMINARIMON

㉗ 梅花亭（柳桥）

一边欣赏在神田川上巡游的带篷游船和柳桥的风景,一边穿过门帘进入店内。里面是完全保留了江户时代风情、创业于明治中期的和果子店铺"梅花亭"。岁月流逝,梅花亭长久以来吸引着人们络绎不绝地前来。产品有精致的高级生果子、三笠山、小福饼等,种类繁多,全部都是师傅们的手工作品。为了保持最新鲜的美味,点心没有使用任何防腐剂,不会对身体产生危害。包装纸的图案也使用了梅花和店名相呼应,礼品盒上面是梅树图案,清新秀逸,十分讲究。去参加茶会的时候,作为礼品送给朋友肯定很受欢迎。

(时) 8:30—18:00,星期六 8:30—17:00 (电) 03-3851-8061 (休) 星期日、节假日 (址) 台东区柳桥 1-2-2 (交) 都营地铁浅草线浅草桥站步行 3 分钟或 JR 浅草桥站、都营地铁新宿线马喰横山站步行 4 分钟 (网) 无

㉗ BAIKATEI（YANAGIBASHI）

Sitting among the scenery of yakatabune (traditional cruising with food and beverages) and Yanagibashi Bridge on Kanada River, is this BAIKATEI. After entering through the noren screen, you will notice the shop, founded in the late 19th century, is full of old elegance. Patrons have long been attracted by its beautifully intricate jo-namagashi, mikasayama (synonymous for dorayaki), and Kofuku-mochi (small daifuku). All sweets are hand-made with no preservatives. BAIKA (Ume or Japanese apricot blossoms) appears on the classy wrapping paper and the gift box. Perfect as gifts for tea ceremonies.

(H) 8:30-18:00, Sat 8:30-17:00 (T) 03-3851-8061 (C) Sundays and Public Holidays (Ad) 1-2-2, Yanagibashi, Taito-ku (Ac) 3-min. walk from Asakusa-bashi Station (Toei-Asakusa Line) / 4-min. walk from Asakusa-bashi Station (JR Line) or Bakuro-yokoyama Station (Toei-Shinjuku Line) (U) N/A

第四章

三色梅最中

以梅花为造型的饼皮,里面是塞得满满的几乎要溢出来的馅料。小巧而丰满的个头,三种颜色的可爱造型"跃然桌上"。白梅里面是豆沙馅,红梅里面是白豆馅,昏黄色梅里面是小仓带皮红豆馅。颜色各异的饼皮和馅料相得益彰。保质期从制造日开始算起,冬季10天,夏季7天。(不同款式1个210日元,3个礼品盒装730日元起)

SANSHOKU UME MONAKA

The Ume-shaped wafers almost overflow with *an*. Small but plump sweets in three colors make the table look gorgeous. Smooth-*an* in white, shiro-*an* in pink, and ogura-*an* in beige. It is typically stylish of them to fill different *an* in different colored wafers. Consume within 10 days in winter and 7 days in summer. (¥210/pc, ¥730/box of 3)

BAIKATEI

㉘ 寿堂（人形町）

洋溢着复古风格的街道上，昭和风情店铺一间连着一间。寿堂创业于1884年，店铺还保留着93年前的模样，传承着历史和和果子的文化。寿堂在每个季节都会创作不同的和果子，经过不断努力，明治三十年（1897年）开始销售的"黄金芋"一下子火了起来。现在更是成为畅销的名点。森井义人设计的刚开始售卖时用来做广告的宣传单，现在成了"黄金芋"的包装袋。店员们非常有礼貌，真诚款待的心意，被代代传承下来。

㊟ 星期一至星期六 9:00—18:30，星期日、节假日 9:00—17:00 ㊡ 03-3666-4804，免费热线 0120-480-400 ㊋ 无 ㊐ 中央区日本桥人形町2-1-4 ㊔ 地铁半藏门线水天宫站直达，都营地铁浅草线或地铁日比谷线人形町站步行4分钟 ㊙ 无

㉘ KOTOBUKIDO (NINGYOCHOU)

KOTOBUKI-DO is the most nostalgic-looking shop in this retro street. Opened originally in 1884, this history-laden building has been handing down wagashi culture for the last 93 years. While earnestly producing different seasonal sweets, they introduced the popular Kogane Imo in 1897 and this has been the biggest seller since. The pattern used on the initial flyer designed by Yoshito Morii is printed on the shopping bag. You will notice the hearty hospitality has also been passed down the generations when the shop staff welcomes you, sitting upright in a formal manner.

(H) 9:00-18:30, Sun & public holiday 9:00-17:00 (T) 03-3666-4804 or 0120-480-400 (toll free) (C) Open 7 days (Ad) 2-1-4, Nihonbashi Ningyo-cho, Chuo-ku (Ac) Less than 1-min. walk from Suitengu Station (Tokyo Metro Hanzoumon Line) /4-min. walk from Ningyo-cho Station (Tokyo Metro Hibiya Line) (U) N/A

第四章

黄金芋

还没有剥开薄薄的黄色糖果纸,就闻到一阵肉桂的香味。拿到手里,软软的糖果让人心生怜爱。烤番薯形状的薄皮里面,是鲜艳的蛋黄馅,用白芸豆和白豆沙加上蛋黄混合而成。馅料和饼皮,还有肉桂,三种香味融合一体,是世间绝无仅有的美味。1 天销售 1500 个以上,一直以来颇有人气。保质期 6 天。(5 个袋装 1000 日元起,礼品盒装 1100 日元起)

KOGANEIMO

Before opening the thin yellow wrapper, you will notice the sweet smell of cinnamon. Inside is a soft small cake in the shape of a sweet potato. Underneath the thin pastry is bright *kimi-an*, a mixture of *shiro-an* and egg yolk. Pastry, *shiro-an* and cinnamon create a delicate savor that is incomparable to anything. More than 1,500 KOGANE-IMO's are sold a day. It is their ever-popular signature sweet. Consume within 6 days. (¥1,000/box of 5; ¥1,100 if you choose the fancy box)

当地人熟知的甜品食堂，品尝花家的手工寒天
EXCLUSIVE CAFÉ TO THOSE IN THE KNOW. TRY HANAYA'S HANDMADE KANTEN

挂着"简餐和甜品"招牌的"花家"，有着七十多年的历史，是在当地相当受欢迎的店铺。菜单中，特别引人注目的是使用了"值得骄傲的寒天"制作的甜品。这里的寒天，原料使用千叶县产的房州石花菜，将其在大锅里面熬煮，再手工切得细细的，完全是自家制作。有嚼劲的口感，沁人心脾的清香，更凸显出冲绳产的黑蜜糖的美味。加入用北海道产的红小豆细心熬煮出来的"赤豆寒天"后，更是让人想要私藏的极品美味。(右页照片是赤豆寒天，480日元)

With a sign that reads "Light Meals and Sweets," HANAYA has been a local favorite eatery for over 70 years. Their most notable dish is their desert with kanten jelly. For preparation of kanten, they use special red agar from Chiba Prefecture. Red agar is cooked in a big pot to extract gelatinous component. The liquid is cooled to set, then cut into fine cubes by hand. The wobbly but chewy jelly with no strong smell, brings out the delightful flavor of muscovado syrup from Okinawa. Kanten topped with carefully cooked and chilled red peas from Hokkaido is so divine that you may want to keep it to yourself. (Mame-kan on the right ¥480)

花家（西日暮里）

(时)10:30—20:00 (电)03-3821-3293 (休)星期二 (址)荒川区西日暮里3-2-2 (交)JR日暮里站步行1分钟 (网)无

HANAYA（NISHINIPPORI）

(H)10:30-20:00 (T)03-3821-3293 (C)Tuesdays (Ad)3-2-2, Nishi Nippori, Arakawa-ku (Ac)1-min. walk from Nippori Station (JR Line) (U)N/A

第四章

小百科 / GLOSSARY

生果子：和果子中的一个分类，多在茶道茶会中出现。生果子多需要现做现吃，保质期较短，含水量在 30%—40% 之间。上生果子是生果子中的高级品，所用食材和外观造型都颇为讲究，口感更为细腻。

半生果子：和果子中的一个分类，含水量在 10%—30%。如最中、石衣。

干果子：和果子中的一个分类，含水量较低，保质期长。如落雁、云平、有平糖、八桥，这些都是干果子中的名品。

门前果子：专门建立在神社或寺院旁的和果子店铺所出售的点心，这种和果子原本只为神社和寺院的参拜者提供。

练切：生果子的一种，以白豆馅和白玉粉为原料。

寒天：琼脂。

蕨饼：使用从蕨类植物的根茎中所提炼出的蕨根淀粉，加入红糖调味，然后经过熬煮、冷却，制作成色泽透明近似凉糕的和果子。

水羊羹：含水量高于普通羊羹，将细红豆沙放入糖水中熬煮后加入寒天，最后倒入容器内冷却凝固成型，其质地很像中国北京的特色小吃小豆羹。

百味供养会：在神坛前供奉百种百味的供品、祈求来年平安无事的日本寺庙神社的传统祭祀活动。

NOTES

东京广域视图

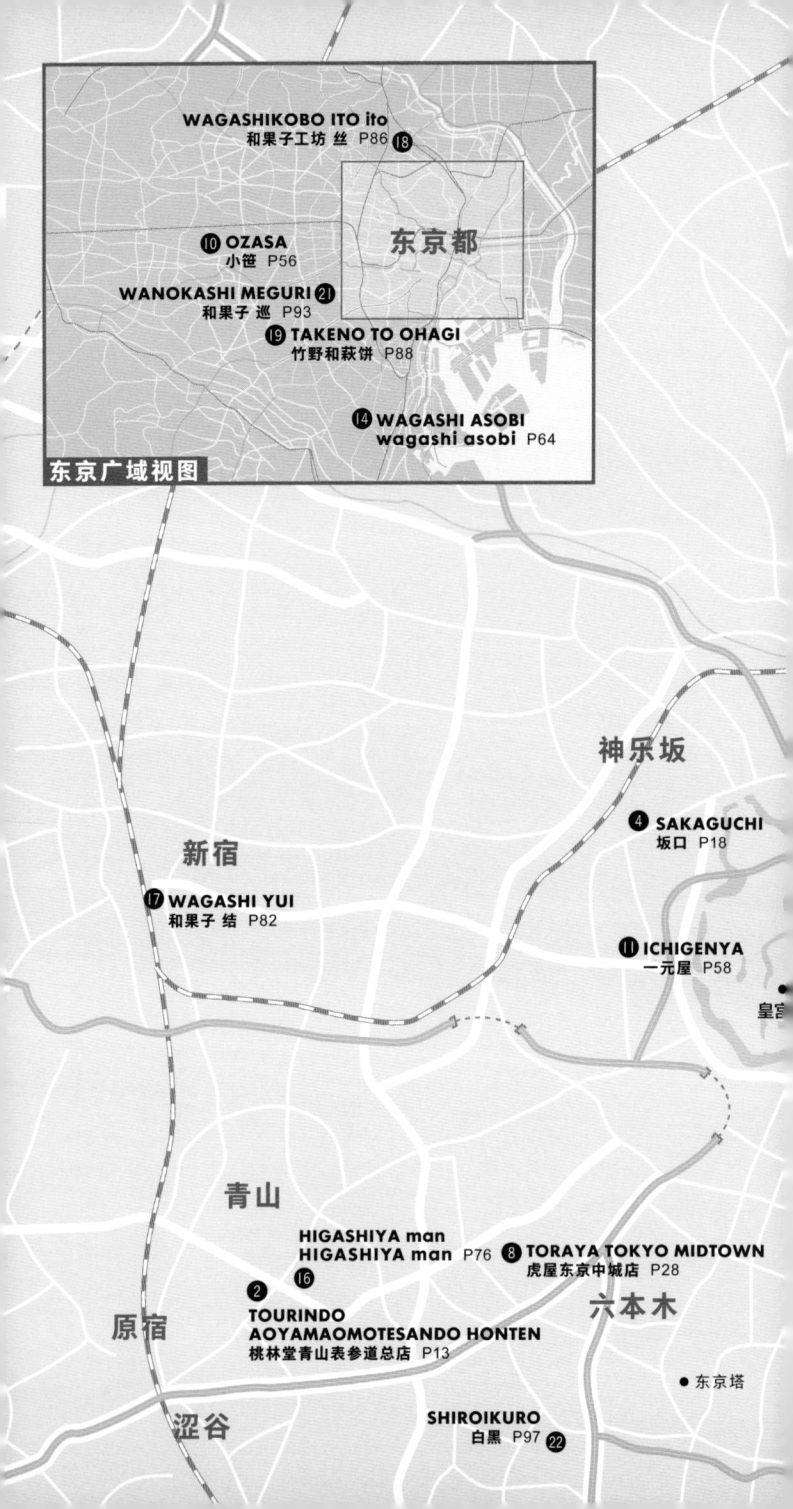

WAGASHIKOBO ITO ito
和果子工坊 丝 P86 ⑱

⑩ **OZASA**
小笹 P56

WANOKASHI MEGURI ㉑
和果子 巡 P93

东京都

⑲ **TAKENO TO OHAGI**
竹野和萩饼 P88

⑭ **WAGASHI ASOBI**
wagashi asobi P64

神乐坂

❹ **SAKAGUCHI**
坂口 P18

新宿

⑰ **WAGASHI YUI**
和果子 结 P82

⑪ **ICHIGENYA**
一元屋 P58

皇宫

青山

HIGASHIYA man
HIGASHIYA man P76

❷ ⑯

❽ **TORAYA TOKYO MIDTOWN**
虎屋东京中城店 P28

TOURINDO
AOYAMAOMOTESANDO HONTEN
桃林堂青山表参道总店 P13

六本木

原宿

● 东京塔

涩谷

SHIROIKURO
白黑 P97 ㉒

日暮里

HANAYA
花家 P120

⓯ KINTAROUAMEHONTEN
金太郎饴糖总店 P69

向岛

KOTOTOIDANGO
言问团子 P16

上野

CHOUMEIJI SAKURAMOCHI ❸
长命寺樱饼 P26 ❼

KURIYA
KASHI
KUROGI
厨点心黑木 P90
⓴

KIMURAYAHONTEN ㉓
木村家总店 P107

浅草

FUNAWA KAMINARIMON ㉖
舟和雷门店 P114

YUSHIMA ⓬
KAGETSU
汤岛花月 P60

● 东京
天空树

● KASHIYA-KOKONOTSU
点心屋九道 P100

NANIWAYAHONTEN
㉕ 浪花家总店 P112

❶ OKASHIDOKORO SASAMA
和果子铺笹间 P10

㉗ BAIKATEI
梅花亭 P116

两国

SEIJUKEN
清寿轩 P110
㉔

㉘ KOTOBUKIDO
寿堂 P118

丸之内

日本桥

❻ NAGATO
长门 P22

银座

GINZA MATSUZAKISENBEI
⓭ 银座松崎煎饼 P62
❾ KUUYA 空也 P54
❺ TACHIBANA 橘 P20

TOKYO ARTRIP WAGASHI by BIJUTSU SHUPPAN-SHA TOKYO ARTRIP Editorial Team
Copyright © BIJUTSU SHUPPANSHA TOKYO ARTRIP Editorial Team, ® Bijutsu Shuppansha
All rights reserved.
Original Japanese edition published by Bijutsu Shuppan-Sha Co., Ltd., Tokyo.
This Simplified Chinese language edition is published by arrangement with Bijutsu
Shuppan-Sha Co., Ltd., Tokyo in care of CITIC PRESS JAPAN CO., LTD, Tokyo

本书仅限中国大陆地区发行销售

日文版工作人员

Cover Illustration: NORITAKE　Designer: TUESDAY (Tomohiro+Chiyo Togawa)
Map: Manami Yamamoto (DIG.Factory)
Photographer: Suguru Ariga (except p32~39, 50~51, 67, 101)
Japanese Writer: You Suzuki (α works)　Translator: Akiko Ebihara Cleaver
Proofreader (Japanese): Mine Kobo　Proofreader (English): Jonathan Berry
Editorial Director: Miki Usui (BIJUTSU SHUPPAN-SHA, CO., LTD.)

图书在版编目（CIP）数据

和果子 / 日本美术出版社书籍编辑部编著；崔江月
译 . -- 北京：中信出版社，2019.7（2019.7 重印）
（东京艺术之旅）
ISBN 978-7-5217-0421-1

Ⅰ．①和… Ⅱ．①日… ②崔… Ⅲ．①糕点 – 商店 –
介绍 – 东京 Ⅳ．① F719.3

中国版本图书馆 CIP 数据核字 (2019) 第 073292 号

和果子

编　　著：【日】美术出版社书籍编辑部
译　　者：崔江月
出版发行：中信出版集团股份有限公司
　　　　　（北京市朝阳区惠新东街甲4号富盛大厦2座　邮编　100029）
承　印　者：北京雅昌艺术印刷有限公司

开　　本：880mm×1230mm　1/32　　印　　张：4
字　　数：83千字　　　　　　　　　　版　　次：2019年7月第1版
印　　次：2019年7月第1次印刷　　　　京权图字：01-2019-2346
广告经营许可证：京朝工商广字第8087号
书　　号：ISBN 978-7-5217-0421-1
定　　价：45.00元

版权所有·侵权必究
如有印刷、装订问题，本公司负责调换。
服务热线：400-600-8099
投稿邮箱：author@citicpub.com